MW01531726

Printed in the United States of America

First Printing, 2012

ISBN-13: 978-1475278231

ISBN-10: 1475278233

Create Space Publishing

www.createspace.com

Table of Contents

Introduction

I n 1977 I was a middle-class 8-year-old kid living in Apollo, Pa. If you don't know where Apollo is, well, join the club. Let's just say it's a little northeast of Pittsburgh. I don't remember much other than snow, bike jumps and the fort in the woods. And an early lesson on how to suck at selling.

One summer afternoon, I decided I needed a nice new pair of Keds. My old ones were shot, and besides, I deserved them because, well, I wanted them.

So I did what any 8-year-old would do: I begged Mom and Dad. Unfortunately, my timing wasn't the best. It was the Wednesday before payday, and, the parental coffers were running low. My parents said they would be happy to toss out my trashed sneaks but I would have to wait until Friday for new ones.

That simply wouldn't do. Those new Keds were calling me like a new Lexus or a killer watch might be calling you right this moment. I had to have the Keds and Friday was just too long to wait. So I dragged out my Radio Flyer wagon, loaded it with old toys and headed out to the cruel world of door-to-door sales. If I wanted new shoes, I would have to get the money myself.

Ding-dong! The neighbor opened her door. (In the '70s kids could roam the neighborhood without a GPS and armed guard).

"Hello," I said. "My parents don't have enough money to buy me a new pair of shoes, and I really want some. Would you like to buy a toy so I can get some shoes?"

Even though my toys were priced at the low, low price of a quarter and sure to be discounted at the slightest resistance, our neighbor said that, no, she didn't need any more toys, even if they were a bargain. Next house? Same answer. Another knock, same thing.

Man, what was wrong with my pitch? How could anyone resist buying toys from me so I could get some new Keds? What was I doing wrong? It wasn't like I was wearing a Dallas Cowboys shirt or something. No way! I was in Pittsburgh Steelers garb like everyone else.

But I wouldn't let a little rejection stand in my way. I could see those Keds on my feet helping me run faster. After about 10 tries I finally got a taste of success. Yes! One toy sold! One quarter closer to my goal. But it wasn't meant to be. My first prospect had called my dad and he came out to escort me home. My selling days were over and sure enough, I had to wait until payday to get my Keds.

So what does that story have to do with you, oh salespeople extraordinaire? You are doing the same thing every day. You are selling like a second-grader.

Lesson 1: You Sell Like a Second-Grader

If you had read the introduction you would know you sell like a second-grader. Let it sink in, and then take a few more seconds to get over what you're thinking: "What the hell does this guy know about how I sell? Who does he think he is? I'm a professional salesperson. I don't sell like a second-grader!"

You do sell like a second-grader and are either A) not listening to yourself or not critically reading your own pitches, or B) the one in a thousand other salespeople look at and wonder how you knock down so many deals. If you are in the A group you really need to read this book. If you are in the B group, you are still going to want to read this book, because there is a ton of other cool stuff you can learn, with research to back it.

There are some good aspects of selling like a second-grader. But unfortunately those bad second-grade habits seem to stick more. If you want the money, new car, nice clothes, security or whatever else motivated you toward the proud, and I do mean proud, profession of sales in the first place, you better pay attention. Face the facts, Junior. You sell like a second-grader. Don't worry though. Now that you know you sell like a second-grader you can use this book to break your bad second-grader habits. You will also get a refresher course on all the good lessons from second grade that you have forgotten.

Would you like some proof that you sell like a second-grader? Think about your last cold call, sales letter or presentation. Bet it sounds a lot like my toy pitch for new Keds. I bet you say something like this:

"Hello, Mr. Prospect, my name is Pat and I'm calling from XYZ Corp. because I was hoping you might have a minute to talk to me about my product. We work with this important company, that important company and the other important company. I would love to show you what we do. Would you have a few minutes? I would love to come meet you."

OK, OK, that example is probably a little too simplistic and my aim isn't to insult you. Truth is I made that example up. It couldn't be that bad, could it? As sure as Keds it can. Here are just a few real — word for word no lie — messages, emails, cold calls and letters from my collection. (What can I say? I'm a sucker for punishment.) You will find them throughout the book, labeled as either a "Crappy Cold Call" or a "Cool Cold Call." Yes, there are some very rare good ones in the pile of crappy ones like these:

Crappy Cold Call: The Confused Caller

"Hi, Chad, this is [Name] with [Company] And I'm calling with regard to electronic editions? I spoke with the receptionist and she said you did have some magazines that have e-editions, but I'd like to talk to you about [Company] technology. (What's due, the car payment or second mortgage?)

You can also visit us at the website which is [Company].com. I'm hoping to hear from you. [Number given], [Name]."

Crappy Cold Call: The "work on my schedule" (and sort of confused) Caller

"Chad, Hi, this is [Name]. I'm with [Company] and I was

calling to introduce myself. I'm not sure if you're familiar with [Company]; we have a product that I wanted to talk to you about — it is a lead-generation, business-development tool (Why would I want to try it if I don't know how it will help me?) *And, um, what I was hoping to do is send you out a free trial for you to test it out. I'm not sure what you use for resources for sales initiatives and business development.* (Didn't you already tell me this?) *However, I did want to forward it to you for tomorrow. If that doesn't end up being a good day, let me know.* (It's on the top of my list!) *The password is only good for one 24-hour session, so I'd like you to use it when you think you have some time. My number is [Number]"*

Crappy Cold Call: The Bully

Hi, Chad:

We're on our second year of the (Conference Name) (Gold star for you!) *This year we want [your company] included as one of the sponsors who will take part in the event. Cost should not be a factor.* (Really? You've seen my budget or can we get it for free?)

As the publisher of record for senior marketing executives in hospitals and health systems, (Company) has the lock on the very desirable end of the target audience you need to engage with, senior marketing leadership. Our marketing programs, which target these executives, bring you through the aware-ness, consideration and preference stages of the sales process. With the addition of the (Conference Name), you're at the point of the sales funnel where your programs come to life and engagements get sold, face to face. Unlike [Other Conference], who we work very closely with, the (Conference Name) goes for a higher-level attendee who typically reports directly to the CEO of the hospital or health system.

Let's talk after you've had an opportunity to review the attached. We want two representatives from [Your Company] at The Art Institute of Chicago on Oct. 15, to be in the midst of 100-plus top award-winning hospital marketers. (Why? Oh, that's right, so we can give you what YOU want.) *I'll call to follow up. Please let me know if you have any questions before then. Thanks!*

Crappy Cold Call: The "creates work for you" Caller:

Hi, Chad,

I am confident this introduction could be a good resource for your team. (Like you really care if I don't think it's a good resource.) *Let me know your thoughts either way.*

We work with two types of companies, providing national video production services and support:

The first being companies and agencies that know they need a reliable national partner for video projects/production.

The second would be companies/organizations that have a video project need and require a reliable partner to make it happen with national or local resources.

Please refer to [Website] for additional information. (That's twice you have asked me to do your job.)

If you see a fit in either of these categories, simply respond to this email and we will set up a short call with one of us to determine if we are a fit.

If not, wish you the best of luck! (Crap! The hex is on if I don't respond!)

Do yourself a favor. Stop reading and go take a look at your latest email pitch to a prospect. Go ahead, I'll wait. See any similarities? Would you love to meet with someone? Introduce yourself? Say "hi"? Don't worry, we will break you of those second-grader habits and give you a refresher course on the good things from second grade that you have forgotten.

You hear the same thing in live pitches, presentations, phone calls and contract negotiations. Some of my personal favorites are preconvention mailings, which incidentally not only look very similar to the emails you just read but have the same second-grader message. The most interesting thing about my collection is that the company I work for is usually exhibiting and not a viable prospect in the first place. Despite that, salespeople are still blindly knocking on my door, kind of like the 8-year-old me trying to get a new pair of Keds.

Crappy Cold Call: The Convention Pitch

Stop by and visit us at Booth 3

Build loyalty, increase market share with unique membership-based CRM loyalty programs and (Name) technology.

Patient relationships depend upon the loyalty of each indi-

vidual consumer. Successful patient relationships are estab-lished and maintained by creating a sense of belonging. Patients need to feel significant to the provider. (Hey, I know, let's lecture them instead of mentioning great client results!) *They also need to be connected to their provider — not just while they are in the hospital, but before and after treatment. Loyalty programs are proven to ensure that an organization becomes the provider of choice within a market.*

(Name) Association is now bridging membership card programs with (Brand) technology, creating a complete marketing strategy package with multiple benefits — streamline patient admissions, decrease data errors and medication interactions in addition to improving ER and first-response information (Yep, this sentence is nothing but product-puke and makes absolutely no sense). *Ask us how we can affordably build or enhance your current marketing program using the latest technology.*

We look forward to discussing your needs in Orlando!

Whew! Can you imagine all of that packed on two-thirds of a postcard? They even had a lady pointing to her head. What does all that verbosity have to do with me and my needs? Absolutely nothing. Why on earth would I waste my time at their booth when I can't even figure out what the heck they are talking about in the first place?

Unfortunately, the second-grade sales curriculum doesn't stop with direct mail. It's prevalent in cover letters of people looking for sales and executive level positions too.

Crappy Cold Call: The Second-Grader Cover Letter

Dear Mr. Rose:

Professionally, I have numerous years of diversified experience and demonstrable results as a senior executive in startup businesses and also the reorganization of existing businesses. (Gold star! Okay, now why are you wasting my time again?)

Some of my accomplishments are:

- *Managed a four-state region for the nation's fifth-largest mortgage banker/multiline financial organization and turned it around to profitability within two months.*

- *Led three multimillion-dollar acquisitions from analysis through negotiations, due diligence, closing and integration of production platform.*

- *Founded multiline financial company which grew from one to 11 branches over an 11-year period servicing over $1.5 billion.*

(Is there a point to this letter? What does this has to do with helping our company?)

- *Researched, structured and managed a multimillion-dollar title insurance joint venture in a three-state region.*

- *Created and managed several real estate and builder joint ventures.*

Enclosed is my resume elaborating on my accomplishments and results: However, a few well-worded statements cannot adequately describe what I have accomplished and what I can do for your company. (And if you don't believe it, just ask him. Dude, really?)

I welcome the opportunity to meet with you and to discuss

my qualifications and how I can be a valued addition. Please call to schedule an interview or contact me via email. (Why do people always want me to do their job? Isn't he soliciting us?)

Gosh, isn't he wonderful? The only thing he left out was "my dad can beat up your dad." This letter came to me, unsolicited. Three times! This guy is asking me for a job, yet all he does is talk about how amazing he is and not about how he can help our company. What's more unbelievable is that after his glorious corporate experience, he became a consultant. No wonder he is now looking for a job. Is he kidding? The icing on the cupcake is his final line: Please call to schedule an interview or contact me via email. Gosh, what an honor — I get to email him. How many of you have written a similar closing line in a sales letter? Be honest!

Let's back up a little. Why do those real examples suck so badly? It all boils down to that powerful one-letter word "I" — the center of a second-grader's world — whether stated or implied, that permeates sales. If you are in sales, you should start looking at "I" as a four-letter word. A filthy habit. You started it in second grade and you still do it now. "I" is the thief who steals your big-screen TV, sports car, kid's college fund or that sweet-ass pair of Manolo Blahniks. "I" is the worst habit learned in second grade. It's the dead weight that pulls you down and sets you back.

I was hoping I could schedule a demo with you. I wanted a few minutes of your time. I'd like to talk to you. I'm hoping to hear from you. I hope you will have the opportunity to attend. I welcome the opportunity to meet with you and to discuss my qualification and how I can be a valued addition. Would you like to buy a toy so I can get some shoes? Ahh, the second-grade school of sales where "I" comes before "you."

Really it's no wonder. Salespeople are under incredible pressure to make goals (some help with that later); they are often working for crappy bosses (juicy stuff about that coming up too); they have to make presentations that make their knees knock (help is on the way); and they play mind games with themselves (seriously, don't you have enough external pressure). We will cover these topics and more, which I'm sure you know because like most readers who size up a book you checked out the table of contents. Or maybe you bought this simply because of the snappy cover. (In any case, thanks!) But let's get back to you.

On top of all those pressures just mentioned, you also have the pressures of paying the mortgage, putting food on the table, buying your kid the latest video console or your wife that Hope Diamond-sized anniversary ring. Sheesh! It can make a salesperson turn to ... well, selling like a second-grader. Face it — even you are guilty of putting your needs before all others in a sales situation. Otherwise, why would you say something silly like: "I wanted a few minutes of your time?"

Don't beat yourself up, kiddo. Not only are you under all that pressure, professionally and personally, to get what you need, but you are also living in an "iSociety." UrbanDictonary defines it as "a society that thrives on products with the letter "i" before them.. But I think the iSociety is the "me first" self-centered society in which we live. According to wordspy.com the definition of iSociety is:

I society noun. A society in which people emphasize independence and individuality.

That's not a bad thing. After all, the United States was conceived on those principles. Life, liberty and the pursuit of happiness has made us the richest, greatest nation on earth. But there should be a another definition too: a society in which personal needs come before all others. Perhaps all the "i" products amalgamate these definitions into self-pleasing, me-first nirvana.

Has everyone been out for their own interests first? Absolutely. Society has always been this way to some extent. But technology has caused it to spiral out of control. Apple didn't start it all with their revolutionary iPod, but it's hard to argue that Apple didn't capitalize on the iSociety and put it into warp drive. Those are a bunch of brilliant dudes in Cupertino, Calif., because they caught the "I" wave at the perfect time and have stayed on the crest. At the writing of this book, Apple had sold 18.65 million iPhones in one quarter!

Instant stardom, get rich quick, secondlife.com, entitlement and mass customization are all part of the iSociety. Individual ring tones, Instagram, YouTube, Twitter, Facebook, blogs, working from home, flextime, DVR, iReport. Instant polls and satellite radio are all part of the iSociety too. The list goes on and on. It's just the world we live in, where people ask for and expect what they want right now. Yes, we love to make ourselves happy, don't we? We want it now and we want to fulfill our needs first. It's cool, almost expected, to let everyone know it.

Which is fine as long as your profession isn't sales. Sure you can have all the "I" crap you want too. What's bad is when this attitude seeps into your sales technique. Your customers live in the iSociety too and they could give a crap what you want. Let the iSociety dominate you like a second-grader on too much sugar and prospects are going to show you the door.

That's why this book is all about you. If you are looking for a guru who talks about how wonderful he is, you won't find him here. That should make you happy, because you want to satisfy your needs first, right? Cool. And that's how it should be. Didn't you plunk down some of your hard-earned cash to get a copy? Even if you didn't pay for it (nice boss) this book should still be all about you.

Herein lays the focus of this book: to break your bad second-grade selling habits and give you a refresher course on your good second-grade habits. If you are selling something, everything you talk about needs to be about your prospect and not "I." There's that word again; "I."

Why is that especially the case in sales? Because deep down, despite the guru nonsense and whatever crap your mission statement might be feeding you about saving the world or helping people live a better life, you are a slave to the iSociety. You want those killer new Nike's and you want them now. You want your kid to go to a great private school. You want the new BMW 3 Series convertible (sweeeet!). Just like I wanted a new pair of Keds in 1977. Not much has changed. Otherwise, why would you put up with all the rejection, canceled flights, cookie-cutter hotels and dinners at Applebee's? It's all about the iSociety.

You might get enough sales to take care of some of your needs, but if you dropped one word out of your mindset you could crush your goals. You could make your sales manager squeal in delight at the prospect of raising your goals even higher next year. (Why do they do that anyway?!)

If it was only that simple. From what I see out there in the sales world, through observing hundreds of salespeople doing their thing, to recording every cold call, to doing tons of research, to learning the secrets of two of the greatest salespeople in the world — my dad and my father-in-law (you will meet them later) — to coaching my own sales team and listening to tape recordings of the bad habits I had, most of us got it all wrong.

This book shares all of that to help you sell more. Chances are there are some things you have never heard before. And here's the thing, by giving you the knowledge in this book, I am serving you. And when I serve you, you help me put my kids through college, replace my broken water heater, buy a new couch and hook up the wife with the latest hand bag. So unless it's absolutely necessary, that is the last you will hear of the "I" who wrote this book. This book is about YOU. I actually tried to write this book without using "I" but it's damn near impossible and drove my editor crazy.

Do you really care what I'm going to do with the money earned from this book? My guess is no. It's the same reason why more people aren't buying from you. You talk about what you want too much. Think about how many times you say "I want" in your process of landing a sale. It's a lot more than you think. What you want is sabotaging deals in your mind. Oh, your mind!

How it can be your worst enemy and affect you, well, just like it did in second grade. We will cover all of that too.

This book will show you how to increase sales more than you ever imagined. You will learn far more than from self-serving gurus and make more money than ever before. On top of it all the lessons are backed not only by years of experience but real scientific research. It's time to break those second-grade bad habits and relearn the good!

Lesson 2: History — It's Gonna Happen

///

*'Tis better to be silent and be thought a fool,
than to speak and remove all doubt.*

—Abraham Lincoln

S econd-graders are wonderful, positive and trusting little beings. Part of their wonderment is the fact that a second-grader believes almost anything. Santa Claus, Tooth Fairy, Easter Bunny or any tall tale told by a friend. Second-graders are master wishful thinkers who believe everything will go their way. That's what makes them delightful to be around and as all parents know, easy to manipulate. Faith, trust and believing everything will turn out OK (also known as illusion of control) are great attributes that continue into adulthood. But relying on them will kill your sales.

Whether you are the new kid on the sales team or a grizzled veteran, chances are illusion of control and wishful thinking are affecting you — you know, a serious case of the gonna happens. Don't sit there and think, "This doesn't happen to me." Second-graders hope things will happen and so do you. Many great men in history did too. Men brilliant in their own right, as you are in yours. Brilliance, however, doesn't mask the fact that tons of studies have come to the same conclusion. When it comes to a "desired outcome" such as winning an election or closing a deal, people tend to be overly optimistic. On the flip side, if it's a bad outcome, people underestimate the chances of that happening.[1] So don't feel bad, you're human after all.

My father-in-law, Russ Serzen, was a great natural salesman and along with my dad had natural intuitive insights into sales. Russ could see all the facets that make a sale work. In the 1970s and early 90s he sold so many orthopedic implants for the DePuy Corp. that he made more money than the CEO of the corporation. Yeah, baby! Straight commission rocks if you have the guts for it!

Before DePuy, he worked as a sales manager for Johnson & Johnson. His group of grade-schoolers, as he called them, sold medical instruments and supplies. Like any sales manager, Russ would ask his 30-odd salespeople what they had in their funnel. When salespeople would tell him, "It's a done deal; don't worry," guess what he did? He worried.

Because Russ knew that once a salesperson convinced himself that a deal was going to happen, wishful thinking would come into play. The salesperson wanted it so badly as to become blind to the variables that could blow up the deal and Russ knew it. To prove his hunch, Russ asked his executive assistant to record for one month each time a salesperson said it was "gonna happen," and if the deal actually closed.

What were the findings of this unscientific study? Only 10 percent of the gonna happens actually closed. That's right, 90 percent of the deals Russ' salespeople were convinced would happen, didn't. What was going on there? Wishful thinking and illusion of control. The salespeople wanted the deals and they wanted them badly. As a result they overlooked the difficulties they would encounter along the way. Then they layered the illusion that they had the variables of a sales deal under control. It spelled disaster. Russ used his findings as evidence that no deal was ever "gonna happen" and just saying it proved so powerful that it made salespeople let up, whether they realized it or not.

One other guy knew a lot about containing the gonna happens — Abraham Lincoln, the 16th president of the United States.

By now, most of you have probably seen Successories, you know those motivational posters and picture frames that were everywhere in the late '90s and are still available today. My favorite is the "Perseverance" poster featuring Abraham Lincoln. The poster says:

"He failed in business in '31. He was defeated for state legislator in '32. He tried another business in '33. It failed. His fiancee died in '35. He had a nervous breakdown in '36. In '43 he ran for Congress and was defeated. He tried again in '48 and was defeated again. He tried running for the Senate in '55. He lost. The next year he ran for vice president and lost. In '59 he ran for the Senate again and was defeated. In 1860, the man who signed his name A. Lincoln was elected the 16th president of the United States. The difference between history's boldest accomplishments and its most staggering failures is often, simply, the diligent will to persevere."

Interesting. Aside from some very obvious historical inaccuracies the premise of this quote is also seriously flawed. First of all his "fiancee" Ann Rutledge was never officially so.[2] And, oops, they also forget that Lincoln won a seat in the Illinois Legislature in 1854.[3] Never mind the successful law firm he built during that time — that would ruin the perseverance poster too. You are supposed to just stare at that poster on your wall and think to yourself, "Well, I've blown tons of opportunities, but one day I will get lucky like Lincoln if I just persevere." That may sell lots of Successories products, but luck will not get you deals — perseverance helps but it's not the magic tonic.

Lincoln was more brilliant than most of us could ever be, which leads to the story of how he became president. Doris Kearns Goodwin's Pulitzer Prize-winning book "Team of Rivals" details

Lincoln's political genius. It's a how-to book on management and winning and you should read it. Kearns goes into fascinating detail on how Lincoln secured the nomination for president. Here is a quick and important summary.

On May 18, 1860, the newly formed Republican Party descended on Chicago and met in a newly constructed hall called "The Wigwam." The party's task was to select a candidate for president of the United States. Back then, delegates from the party had a convention to decide who would represent them. There was no public vote during the primaries, just good old-fashioned party deal making and wrangling. Sure seems more appealing than 18 months of blathering, attack ads and televised debates, don't you think?

The front-runner was William Seward, the popular senator from New York. Salmon Chase, the governor of Ohio, was also considered a front-runner for the nomination, and then there was Abraham Lincoln, the backwoods lawyer who failed at everything (so a "Perseverance" poster could be made to inspire glum salespeople.)

Seward's campaign was orchestrated by the brilliant political strategist Thurlow Weed. Today, he would be viewed in the same light as Karl Rove or James Carville — an expert who had the pulse of the electorate and could get his man elected. Weed was arguably the best of his time, so it's no wonder Seward was confident about his chances.

Salmon Chase had one goal in life: to become president of the United States. As the first Republican governor of a large state, he felt like the office was his for the taking.[4] Despite thinking he had the 1856 nomination in the bag only to lose as result of wishful thinking and mismanagement, Chase didn't see how he could lose when the 1860 nomination came around.

Lincoln, as you know from the poster, had lost quite a few elections. Truth is, had he not lost, Lincoln would have most likely never been elected president or even nominated in the first place. The name he made for himself and the way he handled his losses were the building blocks for the big prize, and Lincoln knew it. He had a plan that he skillfully put into motion to obtain the nomination. It wasn't an accident and he didn't get lucky. Instead he controlled all the variables as much as he could to make sure he won.

To achieve the nomination, a candidate had to secure 233 votes. If after the first ballot there wasn't a clear winner, the delegates would vote again and continue the process until there was a winner. On the first day, after some rules and housekeeping, the delegates were ready to vote. Unfortunately the tally papers wouldn't be ready until the next day, so the proud Republicans had a nice night of wandering the streets, having a meal and then sleeping on every bed, couch and flat surface (even pool tables) they could find.

12 delegates from battleground states stayed at the Wigwam late to see if they could agree on a candidate to oppose front-runner Seward. After two hours of debate, the "Committee of Twelve" had gone in an indecisive circle. Much to his dismay, New York Tribune founder and editor Horace Greeley figured that since there was no consensus it would grease the skids for Seward. Even though Greeley opposed Seward, the editor figured it was a done deal. He wired the Tribune that Seward would be

nominated for president.[5]

About as soon as Greeley made his prediction, things started to come unraveled for Seward. As the night went on, Weed grew more aware of a feeling that some politicians in conservative states may not support Seward after all. Rather than heed the growing evidence supporting his hunch, he continued to insist that Seward was the best man for the job. He was so committed to Seward that it "blinded him to the ... serious doubts that were surfacing about Seward's ... ability to win."[6] And that Horace Greeley would settle an old score with Seward by working against his nomination.

With Seward's nomination train coming off the tracks, Salmon Chase should have been a shoo-in, right? Wrong. Like the first time he tried for the nomination in 1854, Chase didn't have any managers guiding him, didn't try to answer objections to his positions or offer carrots to earn more support. Chase ignored realistic assessments of his chances, instead choosing to believe overly optimistic assessments. He assumed every Ohio delegate would unify behind him without making darn sure of it. "The willful Chase was blind to troubling signs, convinced that if the delegates voted their conscience, he would ultimately prevail."[7] In other words, he didn't control the variables of his nomination. Again!

As a result of Seward and Chase's mistakes, the designation of a clear front-runner got murky. Who could the delegates unite behind? Well, there was that Lincoln guy from Illinois — a good alternate choice , which was just fine with Lincoln because that was exactly what he planned. Lincoln figured Seward supporters would never support Chase and visa versa. The supporters of each candidate needed a second choice and Lincoln was it. Lincoln had also worked harder than the other candidates to amass support of his own which would shock the convention on the first nomination vote. One could argue that had been working toward this political victory his entire career.

Lincoln was careful not to make enemies, even when he lost a previous election to a rival. In fact, some of the people he lost to in previous elections helped him gain the nomination for president. Unlike the other candidates, he didn't reveal his burning desire to become president, and as a result flew largely under the radar screen of criticism and infighting. He assembled a team of supporters to gain support of delegates one by one in each state. Lincoln managed to control the incredible amount of variables that would determine a nominee.

The "Committee of Twelve" continued meeting well after Greeley had wired his prediction to the New York Tribune. The Lincoln team had worked hard to earn the support of the Illinois and Indiana delegates, two of whom were in the "Committee of Twelve." In the early morning, the committee took a straw vote to see if a consensus might emerge. Lincoln came out on top and the real stubborn members of the committee agreed to give up their candidate if he wasn't nominated on the first vote. Lincoln had achieved a key goal. If either Seward or Chase didn't win on the first vote, then the votes would go to Lincoln.

The first tally gave 173½ (beats me how they got a half) votes to Seward, 102 to Lincoln and 49 to Chase, with the remainder of votes for other candidates. Since Chase didn't win, his supporters rallied behind Lincoln, as promised. So did the supporters of other lesser candidates. The second tally gave 184½ votes to Seward and 181 votes to Lincoln. If Seward's folly wasn't Alaska then it sure as hell was the assumption that the support of his delegates was rock solid. To the contrary, it started to crumble. The third tally gave Lincoln 231½ votes, just 1 ½ votes short of the nomination. And that's when Seward's supporters melted away like snow in an Alaskan summer – giving the victory to Lincoln.. By the end of the nomination all those who had voted against Lincoln changed their votes to give him a unanimous decision.[8]

Reflecting on the loss, Seward said: "The leader of a political party in a country like ours is so exposed that his enemies become as numerous and formidable as his friends." What about Chase? According to Kearns, "No doubt he had hoped, and hoped, and hoped against hope … and now came this disastrous, crushing, humiliating defeat." Why did Lincoln win? Kearns puts it best: "Still, if we consider the comparative resources each contender brought to the race — their range of political skills; their emotional, intellectual and moral qualities; their rhetorical abilities; and their determination and willingness to work hard — it is clear that when opportunity beckoned, Lincoln was the best prepared to answer the call."[9]

If you must, go buy the Successories Lincoln poster, but do yourself a favor. Cover up the "perseverance" stuff with the Kearns quote above, especially the "best prepared to answer the call" part. That is the real reason Lincoln won.

He controlled the variables by making enemies friends in case he needed them, by purposely keeping a low profile, and by having a well-oiled election machine ready to pounce when the opportunity came. There was no hoping, wishing or thinking it was "gonna happen."

And it's the real reason why you aren't winning more sales too. You think it's gonna happen. It all comes down to "wishful thinking" and its close cousin "illusion of control." Seward and Chase fell victim to them. Lincoln mastered them.

Wait a minute, weren't we talking about history? What is all this psychobabble mumbo jumbo?! It's the stuff your mind does to you every day that affects your checkbook big time, Buster. It's the same thing that lost Seward and Chase the nomination. Your own noggin will beat you far more than that competitor you hate. Imagine what would have happened to the United States if Seward and Chase hadn't been kicked in the ass by their own brains? Both of them wanted things so badly that their gray matter messed it up, and the same thing happens to you. Still don't believe it? Read on.

You may know "desirability bias" by its more common name: "wishful thinking." "Wishful thinking" happens when you want something to occur so badly that you expect the chances to be higher than they actually are. Like Chase assuming the Ohio delegates would all vote for him, or Weed ignoring bad news about Seward. You know, like that sale you swore was going to happen even though there were land mines you had yet to uncover? Wishful thinker!

Have you ever thought that somehow you will get in a ton of sales right at the end of the year even though your funnel looks like crap? That is wishful thinking. Do you need any more examples? Didn't think so. All salespeople have felt the sting of wishful thinking that never materialized. Bet you are doing a little of it right now.

So how does "illusion of control" play into it? It's basically the illusion that one has control over the outcome of even random situations and it's at the core of wishful thinking. Chase didn't have a well-oiled machine to assure his nomination — he just assumed everything would fall in his favor. Seward assumed no one could touch him because he was a prominent senator from an influential state. Both assumed that even though there were hundreds of delegates who could say yes or no, that the odds would come out in their favor. That is illusion of control.

OK, so we have an example from 1960s and 1860s — here's a more recent example of illusion of control in all its glory. Let's head on over to Las Vegas. When I was just a novice sales kid, my boss John loved Vegas and dollar slots. So when we were there, he would take $300 and plop down in front of a dollar slot machine.

But it wasn't just any old slot machine. John would ask the pit boss which Double Diamond machine was "hot" and toss money at it like a sailor at a strip club. Three bucks per pull, he would play. When he hit a "dry streak" and ran out of cash, he would make me guard the machine while he grabbed another 300 bucks. "You got to feed the machine," John would say. "But she will come around. I know it."

John would play until the wee hours because he knew he had picked the right machine and it was just a matter of time before it lived up to his expectations and showered the pan with the delightful thud of dropping coins. When John won, he would swear up and down it was because he, with a little help from the pit boss, knew how to pick a hot "Double Diamond" machine. When John lost, he would just shrug his shoulders and say "just didn't play long enough." Thinking you can select a machine with randomly spinning reels that will win more than the gazillion other similar machines on the floor: That's the illusion of control.

Go to any casino and see for yourself. From a "hot roller" in a craps game to getting on a streak at the roulette wheel — it's the illusion of control that keeps gambling establishments in the black and people coming back. People swear they can control random odds despite overwhelming evidence to the contrary.

Even though there were similar theories in the early 20th century, the idea of illusion of control wasn't completely fleshed out until Ellen J. Langer, a professor of psychology at Harvard University, proposed the illusion of control theory. Through experiments, Langer discovered that "people who were allowed to choose their own numbers in a lottery game required more money in order to be willing to sell their ticket than did participants who were randomly given numbers." [10] Lotteries are completely random. Even if you pick numbers 1, 2, 3, 4, 5, 6 you have the same chance of winning with those as 12, 15, 28, 35, 48, 7 or any other set of six numbers. Don't worry; you aren't going to be subjected to the hellish statistical equations needed to prove this. Just ask your neighborhood statistician, who will vouch for this — trust me.

Even if people don't choose their own numbers and the winning lotto numbers are randomly chosen, in Langer's experiment people still thought their numbers were better than any other, so much so that a person wanted a premium for the special ticket.

In another experiment people were asked to bet on the chances of hitting a number when they rolled a die. If people were allowed to choose the number on their own, they bet more than if it was randomly assigned to them. Rolling a die is totally random whether the number is assigned or chosen. The illusion of control made people think their personally chosen number had better odds than a random one, even though the odds were the same.[11]

But wait, there's more! Let's say in that same dice experiment a person selects the number six, rolls the dice and gets it. Langer found that if a person has early success in predicting an event — for example choosing a dice number and then rolling that number — the person will have a stronger belief in the illusion of control.[12]

Bet you have seen a new salesperson show up and get a quick sale right out of the gate. Sure, they could just be that good, but chances are it fell into his or her lap. So what usually happens after that? The rookie falls flat and wonders why he isn't getting deals in — after all, the first one was easy. The reason is because that early anomaly of an easy sale made him believe he had control over the variables of all deals without working hard to make sure of it.

So why is this important to you? Because you have lost a ton of deals due to your own illusion of control and your membership in the iSociety. How could that be? You know your product, you have sold it for years and you have seen everything, right? Hate to burst your bubble, but research shows that being more familiar with a task makes the illusion that you are in control even worse.[13] How familiar do you think Seward and Weed were with the political process? Chase had been through the presidential nomination process twice, so he really thought he knew what he was doing.

So does that mean you need to be a pessimist? Not at all. You should, however, recognize your human propensity to be over-confident when it comes to stuff you really want to happen. With the power of that knowledge, you can close more deals.

There aren't very many deals that involve a single person making a decision. If you are in business-to-business sales then you know that everyone, including CEOs, have people they need to check with or answer to. It could be a project director having to run it by the VP or the CEO asking his director for input so no toes are stepped on and everyone feels validated. There could be layers on that too, like a CFO or (gulp) a board of some sort. Or the most dangerous layer of all: that damn competitor you hate who is nosing around in your deal!

Everyone who touches your deal adds a variable. Even in business-to-consumer sales there are layers. A clothing purchase could involve the buyer wishing to check in with the significant other or someone else or wanting to check at the store across the mall before pulling the trigger. Someone might have to check a credit card balance before buying. Or they might just want to "think about it."

So what do salespeople do? They personally control only one facet of all the variables in the deal. They'll say something bone-headed like: "She just needs to check her credit card but she will be back." Or, "I know this deal is going to happen. Jane says she has it all covered and that her VP, CEO, board of directors and the person who is actually going be using what we're peddling never question her decisions. She's only taking that call with the competitor to be polite. This is gonna happen." You ever said that? Don't lie like a second-grader!

Sure, Jane may have told you it's a done deal, but unless you verify with the VP, CEO, board of directors and that user person, plus crush the competitor, you, my friend, are falling victim to the illusion of control and overoptimism. You think you have all those unexplored variables covered because you are special and it's your deal and you really want it and Jane is so sweet and she likes you. Sucker! Second-graders believe in Santa Claus too!

What if Lincoln had followed the same strategy as his opponents? He probably wouldn't have been nominated. Lincoln was smart enough to realize that nothing should be assumed and that the only way to control the variables was to work hard and verify everything. It wasn't perseverance. It was through hard work and not assuming anything that got Lincoln his biggest win. He was also smart enough to judge his chances realistically and "do the arithmetic" to assure a win. You know what's cool? You can be as smart as Lincoln too.

Homework:

1) Just for kicks take an honest look at your funnel in the past year. How many gonna happens actually happened?

2) Look at your current funnel. How much information do you have on each prospect? Learn all the influencers', names, backgrounds and interests. Read the last 10 articles written about that person. Learn your prospects' competitors the same way. Do your research!

3) Come up with five questions you should be asking about each of the influencers of a deal you are working on. What is the CEO's biggest goal? Does your solution satisfy that? Why would your main contact go with a competitor instead of you?

Crappy Cold Call: The "did you see the first crappy email I sent you?" call

Hi, Chad, I was just following up to see if you had received my previous email below. Can you let me know if you have any upcoming research projects we could discuss? Thanks. (No, didn't stand out from all the other crappy, self-serving emails I get from salespeople.)

Subject: Chad, meeting schedule. (The wording is kind of odd, but at least she got to the point in the subject line.)

Hi, Chad, Could we schedule a time in the next few days to discuss your upcoming research projects? I thought you would be interested to learn about a better way to reach real executives for your B2B surveys instead of what most panel providers substitute for it. (I have no idea what this means. Either she shouldn't be contacting me or can't explain how her product can help me.)

As background, clients like Gartner and Forrester have told us that we are exceptional at gathering the knowledge and opinions of true business executives. Our panels were built very differently (the details of how are interesting) and I think you will find our methodology several cuts above anything else. (Gold star! But so what? What does that have to do with my needs?)

Obviously if you are not actively doing anything, then no need for a call right now (just save our contact info) but if you are or will be soon then let's definitely talk. I think you will be fascinated to learn about what is now possible. Thanks, Chad. (I will! Because after this rapt communication, I'm going to invent a reason to work with you very soon!)

Cool Cold Call: Something of value

Dear Chad,

How do you measure the effectiveness of your national sales meetings? What if there was a way to prove that your goals were met? (Sounds interesting, right out of the gate!)

It is the time of year for planning your national sales meetings. (Did I miss some kind of business holiday? This sentence means nothing.) *After the meeting, most sales managers ask themselves, "What did we really accomplish at the meeting and what did we get for that substantial expense?" Start with the Meeting ROI Calculator to determine where your expenses are going.* (Something useful for free is a nice offer.)

What if there was a way to determine if your sales meetings were effective and if your team received the essential knowledge transfer your training set out to accomplish? If you got the help you needed to measure other goals that are important to you and your company, would you take the opportunity? (Gold star! Good question. Who wouldn't?)

[Company] has developed a solution for you — it's called (Product Name). This tool will measure the knowledge each sales

rep acquires from your meeting, thereby dramatically improving your return on investment and holding your team accountable, therefore boosting sales knowledge and performance. (You had me right here! No need to say more, Captain Verbosity.) *Get the most out of your year-end meetings and understand the true value of your meeting.*

We would love to discuss how we can support the success of your 2010 national sales meeting. Please let us know if you would like us to follow up with you in the next couple of days to discuss our solution further to increase your knowledge. (NO!!!! Not the dreaded "we would love." Who cares what you would love? And why do I have to do your job again?)

Wishing you a prosperous 2010!

Grade: B. "We would love" knocks you down a grade point every time, Kiddo.

Lesson 3: 'Rithmetic — What Happens in Vegas Wrecks Sales

///

For a loser, Vegas is the meanest town on earth.
— Hunter S. Thompson

J ust like picking a certain slot machine in Vegas, if you stop with a yes from your main contact and hope you will win, your chances blow. And then you make excuses about why you didn't sell as much as another salesperson. *I have a bad territory. People are tough here. Our product costs too much. WAAAAAAAH!* And you fall into a self-fulfilling prophecy, which we will cover in the next chapter. For now, we are talking about the rosy picture you paint that kills deals.

All deals have layers, and every layer in a deal adds more variability. That's why there are three or more reels on a slot machine, or 38 slots on a roulette wheel — the more reels or slots, the tougher the odds to hit the jackpot. Same goes for craps or any other game in Vegas — there are tons of variables and the house has the advantage.

Everyone knows that you are under constant surveillance in Vegas because the casinos want to make sure people don't cheat. When people cheat, they apply control to the variables in the game and tip the odds in their favor. Being realistic about odds is the first step in winning more sales. Tipping the odds in your favor is the second.

Have you ever played Yahtzee? The simplified explanation is that it's a game with five dice that you roll for different combinations. You get Yahtzee by rolling five of the same numbers in three rolls. For argument's sake, let's say you roll 1, 2, 3, 4, 5 on your first toss. You are going for Yahtzee so you decide to keep the five and roll the remaining dice again. In that scenario, your odds of getting Yahtzee on the next roll are just 1 in 1,296 ($1/6 \times 1/6 \times 1/6 \times 1/6 = 1/1,296$).

Let's wave a magic wand and go back to your second roll again. However, this time around you have two loaded dice that you know will show up as a five. So you have cut the variables of scoring Yahtzee to only two dice. The odds of getting Yahtzee are now 1 in 36 (1/6 x 1/6). Getting better! Load three dice and your odds of getting Yahtzee are 1 in 6. Sweet!

Hypothetically, with all ethical considerations aside, if you wanted Yahtzee and you could pick having three dice you knew would land on a five, or four dice that might land on a five, what would you choose? You would choose the former. In no way is this example given to suggest you cheat in sales. It's there to show how much your odds improve if you forget the illusion of control and actually seize control.

Yes, but there aren't six choices that each person influencing a sales situation can make. It isn't that bad in the real world. Gold star for you! You're right. Influencers of a deal have two basic choices: yes or no.

Say you are selling a widget to a company. Your primary contact is the Director of Widgets who reports to the VP of Widgets who has to run things by the Senior VP of Widgets who signs the contract. That's not all, though. The Director of Widgets isn't going to be actually using the widget. No, that distinction rests with the Widget Coordinator.

The Director of Widgets tells you not to worry about it — it's a done deal. Your "I" and overoptimism take over and you think about that pair of Gucci pumps you've been eyeing at Saks. Screw it! You'll pay full price because you work hard and deserve to spend some of that big commission. All you have to do is stand in front of the fax machine and wait for the agreement to print out into your greedy little hands. Trouble is your odds of closing the deal are probably only 1 in 8 or just 12.5 percent. You are now on the express bus to Payless for overestimating your chances and not controlling the variables.

Say what?! The Director of Widgets said it was going to happen and he is going to make it happen. He wouldn't say that without knowing the VP, Senior VP and Coordinator were all onboard. But with wishful thinking and illusion of control infecting salespeople like the flu, you really think so? The Director of Widgets probably has a severe case of wishful thinking and illusion of control just like Seward and Chase in 1860 Republican nomination, too. Are you going to let that pair of Guccis you want ride on someone you don't know that well who most likely has less control over the process than he thinks? You are going to let your fashion statement ride on 8-1 odds?

And besides the odds, do you actually believe everything your primary contact person tells you? They wouldn't lie to you. Not little old special you. And never would they lie to get you off the phone in a hurry. No way!

Ever heard of sales being a big game? When you think about it, sales aren't much different from Yahtzee. If you want to improve your odds of winning, you have to load the dice. And the only way to ethically do that in a sale is to get a verified "yes" from every person influencing the deal and acknowledgement that you crush your competitor.

Naturally you have heard of the 80/20 rule where 20 percent of salespeople make 80 percent of the deals. Ever wonder what that 20 percent is doing? Perhaps the superstars just work harder. That certainly explains part of the disparity. But superstars also control the odds. They dispel an illusion of control by being damn sure they own the variables, just like Lincoln did.

Forget about wishing for the best and personally make sure all the players are going to say yes. Confirm a yes from two influencers in our hypothetical sales situation and your odds improve to 4-1 or 25 percent. Check three off and your odds improve to 2-1 or 50 percent. Check them all off and you can feel pretty confident that you are going to get the deal. Not "gonna happen" confident, because it ain't done until the ink dries and you get paid, but as close as you can reasonably expect.

Yes, the influence and clout of everyone in the sales process is equalized by the math. If you are thinking that not all sales situations are as clean as that, you're right. The opinion of one person could be weighted. There might be someone in the organization who just carries a ton more clout. Which begs a question: What if you don't investigate that person and assume it's a done deal? Exactly — you could be completely overlooking the gorilla in the room. And skewing your odds toward a loss rather than a win. Better to make absolutely sure.

But Chad, what if I go over the head of my contact and piss her off? Then I won't have any way of getting the deal. There are ways around this dilemma both direct and indirect. If you have gotten to know your primary contact in a sale and earned her trust, there should be no reason why she won't arrange for you to meet the other influencers in the deal. If your requests are met with resistance, then you know you haven't fully convinced your primary contact and your chances of closing are doo-doo.

Once you have met all of the players in the deal, contacting them is fair game. You met them, they listened to you, and now you are simply displaying superior customer service by making sure they were satisfied with what you presented, and if not, how you can adjust to meet their needs. If your primary contact gets his skivvies in a twist over it, then you know he is a control freak, paranoid, on the bubble or has little influence in the final decision. In other words, you know there is more information to be discovered. You also know you should take what your primary contact says with a grain of salt.

Sometimes though, the person who is influencing the deal may be a moving target or a complete enigma. A client of mine once told me about her COO who was nicknamed "Lucifer" because she wouldn't even give employees the time of day. Even if you were selling the meaning of life, she probably wouldn't see you.

You may also get word "from the top" that all decision making has to go through your primary contact. So what does a Gucci-loving salesperson do in a situation like that? Question the dickens out of your primary contact, in a friendly "hey, I'm just trying to help you get what you want [which, of course is the wonderful product I sell]" way.

It's a lot more than just asking, "Did they like it?" It gets down to asking detailed questions: "What did you tell Lucifer about how our widget would help your company exceed goals?" ... followed up by something like: "And what was her response to that?" Or: "What ways of using our widget did she come up with that you hadn't thought of?"

You want open-ended questions that really dig out the truth and make your primary contact think about what to find out at the next meeting with the Prince of Darkness. This helps you zero in on the real interest level and if your contact has actually sold it up the ladder. If you realize your primary contact hasn't done this, then you need to offer specific, actionable strategies to convince the other players in the deal to say yes.

But I can't get to the CEO or the VP. They will never take my calls. They will if you have something smart to say or if you get the correct person to contact them for you. This is the time to use your sales VP for what he was created for: doing anything legal and ethical to help you land deals. Creating sales quotas, asking for reports or asking when the deal will come in is sales manager bullshit (we will get into that later). Sitting down and strategizing with you, making the calls to help you and working to forge relationships with your prospects' upper management is the only reason why your sales manager should get a cut of your action. Period.

One of those ways is by forging strong relationships with prospect upper management right from the start. The best way is for your VP to be well-known in the industry by serving on boards, writing articles, speaking at trade shows or sending out useful knowledge to prospect brass. Doing all of those things gives your boss a better chance of schmoozing with your prospect's bosses.

Even if your VP is a slacker and doesn't do any of that stuff, there is still a pretty decent chance of hooking up with a prospect VP by phone or personal visit. VPs tend to be more open to meet each other than you – it's a battle-scarred, paid-your-dues camaraderie I guess. Trying to figure out why is about as useful as worrying about why dogs sniff butts when they meet, but, hey, they do it. It's pretty much the same thing with VPs and CEOs.

Your boss should be asking the prospect's boss how things are going with the selection process, what their golf score is and if they are ready for happy hour — in other words checking that variable off your list. By no means does this mean your boss should play car lot sales manager and say "What do we have to do to get it done today?" even if you sell cars for a living. Joking aside, it means your boss provides a higher "peer-to-peer" facet of information to your deal. If handled correctly, this can really work in your favor.

Where do salespeople fail the most in controlling the variables? When responding to RFPs or requests for proposal. The number-crunching antisocial dorks who churn RFPs out of corporate basements love to say that you shouldn't contact anyone. And wishful thinking salespeople actually listen to them. *It said not to call and I didn't want to piss anyone off. It was a good RFP, we answered all the questions and added a really shiny cover. I feel good about it.*

Have you ever asked the people who use your products what they think about RFPs? They hate them as much as you do! If you don't contact those people during the process, ask intelligent questions and offer useful information, you are playing spreadsheet roulette with the number-crunching dorks in purchasing. And no matter what the RFP says, the only thing those dorks are going to look at is the cost.

If you get in touch with all the influencers in the deal you have a much better opportunity to survive the cost comparison. Your odds of closing if you chalk up an RFP to illusion of control are next to zero, especially if you know you cost more than your competitors. But you would never just send in an RFP and hope for the best, would you? That's what your lazy competitors do, right? The reason is you know you will not win an RFP simply by answering the questions and hoping for the best. Prospects hate them as much as you do, so bend the rules and see how many more of them you score.

But wow that sounds like a lot of work and I'm really busy making more appointments. If you can control the variables and ditch the wishful thinking, you won't need as many prospects to make your numbers!

Why do people say "sales is a numbers game?" Anyone who can afford to burn through leads, raise your hand. Anyone who has said, "Oh, losing a few deals is OK; I will just dig up more prospects and fill my funnel," send me $100. Assuming you answered honestly and this book sold a bunch of copies it's time to order my personal jet — carbon footprint be damned!

Why do we say things like that? Is it because we have been hearing that same crap forever? Have you ever stopped to think how stupid that notion is? Sales is a numbers game implies that qualified prospects are like biscuits at the Shoney's all-you-can-eat breakfast buffet. Don't worry, they'll make more. In fact, there are companies in existence just to sell "qualified sales leads." Where do those grow anyway? How is it that there is an unlimited supply? Fact is good prospects are more like a discounted HDTV at a Black Friday sale — you need to elbow your way in to get one.

And yet you will hear it at sales meetings across the country. Sales is a numbers game. Fill the funnel! And John used to say he needed to feed the Double Diamond to get it to hit. Just like gambling money and discount HDTVs, your prospects are limited. You must treat each one like a precious gift. Let your competitors play the numbers game. You play the control game.

The only numbers game you should be concerned with is how much you can increase your odds of closing a deal. If you can control the variables and aren't afraid to do the 'rithmetic, you won't need to waste time on a giant funnel because your closing ratio will soar. Or you can continue to sell like a second-grader and hope it will happen — which will lead to another nightmare: the self-fulfilling prophecy.

Remember when we talked about Yahtzee and controlling variables a few pages before? Well, here's a handy little chart to help you do it yourself. Variables on the Y axis, Variables controlled on the x axis — Find the intersection of the variables compared to how many variables controlled to learn your true chance of closing. Finally you can shake the *gonna happens!*

Number of Variables	1	2	3	4	5	6
1	100%					
2	50%	100%				
3	25%	50%	100%			
4	13%	25%	50%	100%		
5	6%	13%	25%	50%	100%	
6	3%	6%	13%	25%	50%	100%
	Chance of Close					

Homework:

Score all of your prospects based on the RoseClose matrix above. Do you have more or less work to do to close your deals?

Crappy Cold Call: Letter from Tolstoy

Hello, Chad,

Hope you are doing great. My name is [Name] and I am with [Company].

It gives me immense pleasure informing you that our VP Sales, [Name], is scheduled to be in Arizona tentatively on 3rd and 4th February, 2010. (You mean so he can tentatively schedule his trip?) *I wanted to check your availability for a meeting with him. The agenda of the meeting is to introduce our company / services and answer your questions regarding possibilities of [Company] supporting your Software Development, QA/Testing, Remote Infrastructure Management Services and Back Office Processes on a remote basis.*

As a brief introduction, [Company] is a 12-year-old, CMMI Level 4, global IT services company, specializing in the delivery of dual-shore services in the areas of Offshore Software Product Development, QA / testing, RIM and KPO. (Say what? Speak my language already! Tell me how you will grow my business, not how long you have been in business and how wonderful your company is.) *With over 1,500 engineers, we provide services to startups, mid-sized and multi-billion dollar companies. As the recipient of the prestigious CNBC – ICICI "The Emerging India" award in the ICE & ITeS category for the year 2007 and Winner in the Deloitte's Technology "Fast 500 Asia Pacific" Program for 2007 and 2009 and having been placed amongst the 50 best companies to work for in India for 2009 in a study conducted to identify great workplaces across the country, we are recognized as an established organization in the Software Services and Process Outsourcing industry.* (Clearly he has read "War and Peace" or gets paid by the word. Or both.) *Currently, [Company] is providing a suite of outsourced services to global companies throughout the North America, Europe, Africa, Australia and Asia.*

We can help you to face your IT challenges through our range of services including:

- *Application development, testing, enhancements and maintenance (Client-Server, Web, Mobile applications, Interactive applications, Legacy applications, etc.)*
- *Software product development and testing (New development, Version upgrades, deployment/implementation, Platform/Stack, etc.)*
- *Ecommerce, Web/Mobile portal design, development, testing, enhancements, integration to billing systems, back-office supply chain and financial applications*
- *Quality Testing & Assurance (As an independent service for applications & software products)*
- *Remote Infrastructure Management services include (Desktop Management, Network Management, Security Management, Server Management, Helpdesk Services)*
- *KPO Services (Market Research, Legal Processes, Web based technical and non-technical support, etc.)* **(This is an impressive list, Tolstoy, but it makes no sense if you don't show how it will help me make or save money.)**

We take pride in the fact that we have consistently outperformed our clients' most demanding requirements and exceeded their expectations with regard to performance, process improvements and relationship management, with our unique model of engagement, Extended Team Model. Today, 15 out of the 100+ clients that we have consider us to be their strategic partner and many have been with us for six years or more. We have taken multiple clients offshore and believe that we possess the experience, process depth, technology skills and the right attitude/ commitment to make this relationship a success.

With this as a background I want to request, if you could spare some time for [Name] to expand on this introduction and discuss possible technology partnership involving present and / or future technology initiatives that you/ your company might be considering.

I look forward to your response and confirmation on a suitable date / time schedule that would be convenient for you, for our meeting. (Seriously, do you think I made it this far? And why would I respond, anyway?)

Cool Cold Call: Short and Honest. STOP READING RESUMES!

Reading resumes in your inbox takes time and it's easy to miss a great person!

Don't judge a book by a cover and don't settle for a stack of resumes. (This is true. They have my attention. And no lies about "hoping you're well.")

The solution — screened and prepared resumes.

We offer annotated resumes with salary history, reasons for leaving past positions, gaps in employment, and key business accomplishments!

The experts at [Company] can assist on a wide range of positions: administrative, accounting, technical/IT and professional. (So, they got my attention and gave me a great solution and now show they are the perfect choice. Sign me up!)

Keep in mind we offer a flat 15 percent direct hire fee with a 100-day replacement guarantee.

STOP looking at stacks of resumes and call us at [Number]

Visit [Company].com to learn more about us. (That sounds

fantastic! Yes, they want me to do their job, but the offer is so cool, I just might. If the salesperson had called (which he didn't) it would have been a lock!)

Grade: A. Even though they asked me to call, the reason was compelling and the email was short, to the point and offered a solution to help me.

Lesson 4: Social Studies — Belly-Up Banks and Rice Famines

//

We are a collective victim of violence.
—Alan Schwartz, then-Bear Stearns CEO

*T*he northeast territory just isn't very good. We're over-priced in the market. I just can't seem to get through on the phone. Prospects don't want to take my calls. Have you ever heard things like this bantered around your company? Worse yet, have you ever said anything like that? Say it isn't so!

Don't beat yourself up if you have. So have countless other people. Fact is what you have fallen victim to has destroyed economies and erased fortunes so why would you be immune to it? It's the self-fulfilling prophecy. W. I. Thomas put forth the modern theorem that "if men define situations as real, they are real in their consequences."

Think about that for a minute. "If men define situations as real …" doesn't mean the situation is real, you just *think* it's real — your mind has convinced you. "They are real in their consequences." So when something goes wrong or right (the consequence), you have something to attribute it to: the situation you made real in your mind. Put another way, by a much smarter guy than me, "The self-fulfilling prophecy is, in the beginning, a false definition of the situation evoking a new behavior which makes the originally false conception come true." [14]

The guy who said that was Robert K. Merton in a breakthrough essay on "The Self-Fulfilling Prophecy" published in The Antioch Review literary magazine in 1948. Merton devised a story of the fictional "Last National Bank" as an institution that was ruined because of a self-fulfilling prophecy. Last National like hundreds of banks that failed during the Great Depression was doing just fine until a rumor started to circulate that it might be insolvent when, in fact, the bank was solid. That rumor spread and pretty soon more people showed up to the bank to withdraw their money before it was too late. That just led to more and more people showing up and the bank eventually running out of money and, guess what? Going belly up.

The belief or prophecy led to the ruinous outcome for Last National. Had the prophecy not started, the bank would have remained solvent. Too bad this situation isn't just fictional. Fast-forward to 2008 and Bear Stearns and its rapid descent into oblivion fueled by self-fulfilling prophecy. The company had ridden the gravy train of subprime mortgages, more specifically by issuing securities backed by those mortgages. As you know, the housing balloon popped and Bear Stearns investors got a little nervous. Were there enough liquid funds to allow them to cash out? Bear's CEO Alan Schwartz assured the public that, yes, there was: $17 billion. But that wasn't enough to staunch the hemorrhaging caused by one nasty little word: rumors.

Had Bear's liquidity dried up? Better run over there and grab cash while you can. One panicked investor led to another, then another — and that led to a jittery rolling snowball of fear wanting money. It was a crisis of confidence. "A good old-fashioned bank run."[15] Would Bear have survived the mortgage meltdown if not for this self-fulfilling prophecy? It's hard to say. But one thing is for sure: The self-fulfilling prophecy ruined one of America's most storied investment banks and it took Morgan Stanley backed by the government to salvage what was left of Bear. Said Schwartz, "We are a collective victim of violence." Self-fulfilling prophecies will victimize your sales career too if you don't watch it.

Prophecy is a distinctly human undertaking that can be especially dangerous in emergency situations. Every city and state in the country has a disaster plan and in that plan there are outlined procedures for what is called "rumor control." Rumor control is a coordinated government effort to snuff out any false prophecy before it becomes fact in the mind of the populace during a crisis.

Florida has its share of emergencies with the annual hurricane conga line that marches toward the state seemingly year after year. When it comes to rumor control, the state's protocol is pretty clear: "Further, any rumor that isn't addressed within a day becomes a 'fact,' resulting in a far more difficult challenge of mitigating the perception of authorities covering up or withholding information."

Hurricane Katrina and the resulting situation at the Louisiana Superdome deliver a striking example of how such rumors can run rampant, agitate a populace and even distort perceptions of the very news outlets we rely upon for accurate information. If you recall, there were reports of rapes, hundreds of dead and even a sniper in and around the Superdome and the Convention Center in the aftermath of this massive hurricane.

Even Mayor Ray Nagin, granted not the most gifted of leaders or politicians, declared on "The Oprah Winfrey Show" that people had been "in that frickin' Superdome for five days watching dead bodies, watching hooligans killing people, raping people." In fact, little of what was said about the Superdome was actually true — only 10 bodies were found in the Superdome and four in the Convention Center, not hundreds. The rumors started inside the dome and spread like a virus amplified worldwide by mass media.

Those untrue reports made people even more hysterical. The self-fulfilling prophecy was coming on strong. Those rumors of chaos in the Superdome had the effect of "undermining [Nagin's struggle to keep morale up and maintain order."[16]

Imagine a disaster hitting the United States and unlike Hurricane Katrina the government was on-site without delay with plenty of food, water and shelter. What if a rumor started that food and water were running low? People would rush to get as much food and water as they could and in the end supplies would indeed diminish and perhaps even run out. Many would argue that it's the "crowd mentality" that causes such breakdowns and prophecies to come true.

Mid-2008 the media started cranking up again. This time it was breathless reports about food shortages. We were on the brink of running out of food! Especially rice! Never mind that organizations like the USA Rice Federation said that there was no shortage in the U.S.[17]

Yes, in developing and poor countries stocks of rice have been cut in half, but in the U.S.? Nope. That is until the panic set in. Just in case the news reports were actually true for once, people made a run on rice. Better stock up just in case! And guess what that led to? Higher prices, rationing and, yikes, shortages!

But not shortages of all kinds of rice — just the brands immigrants like in the big ol' whompin' bags.[18] People freaked out from New York to Alaska where 200 people lined up in front of an Anchorage Costco to lug out 50-pound sacks. Shoppers could get smaller packages at lots of other places in town, but that wasn't the point. Said one rice hoarder: "[Having rice] is showing you're not poor. It's a mental thing. My mom, she's Chinese, she compares it to money. I got rice. I got money."[19]

No big deal. It's just rice. Well consider this: In 1943, Bengal, under British rule at the time, had a problem with rice. A cyclone hit and supposedly damaged rice crops, plus rice was being shipped off to feed British soldiers — but despite all of this, crops were strong and production was higher than in 1941. So how did an estimated 3 million people starve to death in the Bengal famine? Rumors and rice hoarding which led to huge price increases.

Rice became a killer investment and rice growers and speculators got rich off the hysteria. What really killed all those people wasn't a lack of rice but the panic-induced price run-up that made it unaffordable to the poor. Huh, I wonder if that happened in 2008, too?

Research has shown, however, that a self-fulfilling prophecy doesn't need crowds as a catalyst to fruition. It can happen in one-on-one relationships and certainly in your own mind. Merton stated that "self-hypnosis through one's own propaganda is a not infrequent phase of the self-fulfilling prophecy."[20] Remember Russ, my father-in-law? He put self-fulfilling prophecies to the test as a car shopper.

Russ loved cars. He was monetarily conservative but when it came to cars, oh, baby, would he snap out a checkbook! But Russ was also a seasoned sales pro who liked to test salespeople — it was sort of a sport for him. There are some excellent car salespeople out there but, let's face it, most of them are horrible. Every few years, when Russ was itching for a new car, he would slap on the rattiest shorts he could find, a worn-out T-shirt, some 99-cent Walgreens flip-flops and tool on down to the Jaguar or Mercedes dealer.

Since showing up in his current high-end car would tip the salespeople off, Russ would park by service and then walk around to the showroom. Most of the time he got very little help — he was just some bum off the street who couldn't buy a car anyway. And when he looked around and left after no one had approached him, surely the salespeople would think, *yep I was right, the guy had no money. No use talking to him. It would have been a waste of time.* That's a personal self-fulfilling prophecy. Ever looked at a name or business on a phone list and thought: *They will never buy, no need to call them.* I know I have. It's the same thing.

Every now and then, Russ would stumble on a salesperson who didn't let his mind get in the way of his wallet. It was usually a new guy who just wanted to make some money and was going to keep trying until it happened and hadn't been around long enough to create self-fulfilling prophecies. Remember when you were hungry like that? I hope you still are. Anyway, when that smart salesperson looked past the package and the prophecy, Russ would reward the person with a sale and a check to pay for it.

The sales territory, the bad part of town, the business with a ratty paint job or the ratty guy buying a car — we have all had our share of self-fulfilling prophecies. Sure, you may go ahead and make a few half-assed calls into that "crappy state" and you may go ahead and walk into the business with the ratty paint job, but are you really giving it your total effort? Hate to be the bearer of bad news (or the truth, depending on how you look at it) but you don't give it your all because deep down you have already convinced yourself it's going to turn out poorly.

In my experience, the older the salesman, the worse the disease. You get kicked around for 20 or 30 years selling stuff and you might feel the same way too. My dad, who sold Pennzoil motor oil for darn near his whole life, somehow managed to keep self-fulfilling prophecies from getting the best of him. I'm sure he had his bouts with it, but he kept going after every prospect and believing he could sell them no matter what. It's part of the reason why he sold more motor oil than most people and expensive motor oil at that — and isn't all motor oil just the same as well oil?

Not Pennzoil. It was the most expensive oil in the market. There were other salespeople who whined about oil being a commodity and that it was impossible to sell it for a premium because people were just going to buy Castrol, Valvoline or something cheaper, but not him. Why dwell on it? As long as he sold Pennzoil he was going to be the most expensive and as soon as he let that self-defeating commodity bullshit get in his head the self-fulfilling prophecy would start.

Well, I tried to sell it but we are the most expensive and oil really is oil, and we cost more so its almost impossible to sell! To the contrary, my dad embraced that it was more and used it to his advantage. Pennzoil was worth it and he believed it.

When he showed up in Tampa, his final territory before retirement, Pennzoil had a meager $45,000 in sales. In the first year, he signed up 11 new car dealers in this "dog" territory to the tune of $1,155,000. By year five he hit 33 new dealers with $6,270,000 more. But wait, there's more! He also secured 20 new independent lube centers for another $1,800,000 in new business. *High-priced oil. A real* commodity. When he left it was the top territory in the nation.

Among many things that made him a success was first surveying car dealers to learn about their needs. Imagine that? Before he started puking product at prospects my dad actually asked about the prospect's needs. Then he prioritized them and found a solution for each of those needs. He also killed the self-fulfilling prophecy that Tampa was a bad territory.

Finally he resisted the urge to devise a self-fulfilling prophecy that he wouldn't win because oil was oil and the cheap stuff would win out. Commit yourself to facing your sales demon and you will not only beat it, you will excel in sales too. Promise. What kind of sales bullshit are you feeding yourself? Spit it out and push the plate away!

In his article, Merton lays out a plan for beating a self-fulfilling prophecy. "The initial definition of the situation which has set the circle in motion must be abandoned. Only when the original assumption is questioned and a new definition of the situation introduced, does the consequent flow of events give the lie to the assumption. Only then does the belief no longer father the reality."[21] Sounds simple enough — just stop believing what you thought was true as if you were watching an episode of "Criss Angel Mindfreak."

It takes hard work to avoid creating self-fulfilling prophecies and if you don't commit to the task, you are screwed. James Loehr's best-selling book *Stress for Success* outlines the story of how Loehr helped Olympic gold medalist Dan Jansen shake the incredible mental baggage he carried as a result of the of the events at the 1988 Calgary Olympics. The day of his best event — the 500 meter — he learned that his beloved sister died. Jansen decided to skate anyway and fell during the race. Then during the 1,000 meter race, he fell again.

After the Olympics, Jansen regained his champion form and even broke the 500 meter world record not once but twice. Then came the 1992 Olympics in Albertville, France, when the media brought up the death of his sister and asked if he could shake it. He couldn't, finishing fourth in the 500 meter and 26th in the 1,000 meter. Jansen turned to Loeher and his team for help and they put him on an intensive mental and physical program so Jansen could shake the demon of his sister's death.

Part of that program was to keep a training journal that tracked 27 variables. Those 27 variables were tracked every day for more than two years to help break his cycle of Olympic defeat. As they prepared for the 1994 Olympics in Lillehammer, Loeher noticed that Jansen talked about how much he disliked the 1,000 meter. Jansen never believed he would win it and as a result he never had and if that isn't a self-fulfilling prophecy, I don't know what is.

Six months before the games started, Loeher asked Jansen to start writing "I love the 1,000, I love the 1,000" across the top of his training log. Jansen wrote the words roughly 180 times and each time he did, it made him think the opposite of his belief. Eventually Dan Jansen started to like the 1,000 meter and in his final opportunity to win an Olympic gold medal, he did it in the 1,000 meter. Was it simply writing the affirmation all those times that changed his prophecy? No, it was the slow progression of actively thinking the opposite that did it — writing was just the vehicle to make him stop and do so. And yes, it took a lot of writing.

You can do that too. Hate making dials? Write "I love the phone" on a sticky note before you leave the office and stick it on the handset. When you start your day, write it again and get dialing. Don't like a territory? Find one cool thing about your territory and write it down in your journal every day. Hate what you sell? Quit brother, I can't help you.

Look, Dan Jansen overcame the power of *death*, by doing this. You mean to tell me you can't overcome feeling like your product costs too much? Of course you can.

Homework:

1) This week write down all the excuses your fellow salespeople say. Then listen to yourself and write those down too.

2) Find a way to defeat your worst self-fulfilling prophecy first. Maybe you need to write down the opposite of the prophecy every day when you start and then have it crawling across your screen-saver. Once you have conquered the first one, move on to the next.

Crappy Cold Call: You are so rude!

Good Morning,

We recently sent you an email informing you about our [Trade Show], but haven't heard from you. (Maybe you didn't hear back because you had nothing useful to say. Like this time!?)

Kindly let us know if you would like to receive more information about the event. (Awww...seems someone is a little frustrated after just one crappy email. Remember, oh salesperson you are trying to sell me. Working with you isn't my cross to bear.)

Have a good day, thank you
[Salesperson]

Cool Cold Call: The Relevant Story

Dear Chad,

The best choice for that job you plan to fill may be someone you already employ. (WOW! A bold, interesting statement to catch my attention.)

Although that individual may be your most optimum candi-

date, it is possible that you might be disregarding him or her due to lack of education or experience.

Several years ago, [Company] assessed an hourly rate production supervisor for [Client] of Pampa, Texas. His assessment results indicated he would be a great candidate for outside sales. The general manager laughed at such an outlandish recommendation since the test taker lacked a college degree and had no prior experience in sales.

Yet in a little over a year when the company could not find an experienced salesperson either from within the company or from the outside to take the job of parts sales for the Louisiana, Mississippi, and Arkansas territory, they decided to give him a chance since no one else would take the job.

He not only succeeded, but he excelled in the job. Some twenty-two years later (after that division of [Company] had been sold to [Company]) he retired as the number one drilling rig salesman in the world for [Company]. He accomplished this with no college degree, no formal sales training, and none on the qualifications that the company had previously required to be considered for a job in sales for [Company].

The [Product] assessment provided by [Company] was the key in recognizing the raw potential talent in this candidate; he was scored higher than average mentally, indicating more than the required level of mental ability to complete a college degree program though he had not. **(This masterfully connects the success story to the solution they are selling. I want this!)** *Further, he was above average in all of the other mental aptitude traits that are often pre-requisites for successful achievement in sales. Behav-*

iorally, [Company's] assessment observed that he had excellent energy and drive combined with high self-esteem and the internal desire to win, excel and succeed. These outstanding traits and their levels combined with his assertiveness and incentive-based orientation to win all added up as excellent motivators that would allow him to be able to meet and deal with people well and to successfully sell them the company's products and services. (This story paints a picture of why I should spend money for such a solution. Notice he didn't tell me, he showed me!)

We feel sure you have existing employees whom just might have that outstanding future capability with you that you, for whatever reason, have not been discovered yet. We encourage you to have them take an [Product] assessment so that you might discover, independently and objectively, just what their true capabilities are in your organization. (Assuming carries risk, but this is a safe assumption. There could be hidden talent in any company.)

We provide the [Product] and its sister version, the Sales [Product], what are considered "the gold standard in America," to employers of all sizes and types across America. With each report whether compiled on an existing employee or applicant, employers have the option to receive the following Management Summary which optionally may include a Hire / No Hire Recommendation based on the job and the requirements.

To view a sample [Product] report and a sample Management Summary visit [Website]

This report is just as valuable in the selection process as it is determining what you really have in the strengths of the people you now employ.

The [Product] is just $125.00 with the Management Summary. If you are not pleased with our report – YOU OWE US NOTHING. (And I get to try it with no risk? Kick ass!)

May I suggest you try the [Product] report today to provide you additional insight into people you currently employ and applicants as well? (Only after delivering a compelling story of success and describing how it will help me does he talk about "I." This guy is good.) *You have absolutely nothing to lose! You will find more information on testing and assessments at [Website].*

Call me and I will answer any questions that you may have. (Rats! Don't tell me to call you. Suggest some times or tell me when you will call. Fish don't reel themselves in. You have to do it!) *We will get you set up to try out this incredibly accurate assessment that can help you increase sales, develop better supervisors / managers, provide insight you need for succession planning, and serve a variety of other valuable purposes.*

Cordially,
[Salesperson]

Grade: B+. Asking me to do his job cost some points. And even though the stories were compelling, the email was far too long.

Lesson 5: Music — Sorry Slick

///

They love to tell you, "stay inside the lines."
But something's better on the other side.
— John Mayer

Most likely no matter where you went to elementary school, you had music class. If you have kids and are in a good school district you have been to a "concert" or two to see your kids sing, play the recorder or some other instrument badly but with lots of chutzpah. Chances are there won't be a kid up there who doesn't look as if he or she is having a great time. When you are a second-grader, standing up there and singing your heart out is downright cool no matter if you have a voice or not. Where else can you spend 10 or 15 minutes standing in front of people and get praise for an entire night? Well, in sales of course.

When you're a second-grader, there's no such thing as stage fright. Mom, Dad, Grandma your teacher and whoever are smiling and clapping and telling you how much you rule — that's all that matters. Most 8-year-olds can sing songs from memory even while doing dance moves and look like they are having fun doing it. Children are taught music and asked to perform because it instills confidence and improves development. Come sixth grade though and that requirement vanishes (at least at our school). Maybe it's because kids at that age are more self-conscious or simply want more extracurricular choices. Think back and unless you were one of the kids who chose a performing art through middle and high school, I bet you started to feel more and more self-conscious.

Up until now this book has had you speeding down the scold highway — stop selling like a second-grader or in the corner for you! That's over (at least for now) because you need to let your freak flag fly like a second-grader singing "The Twelve

Days of Christmas" with synchronized choreography. Otherwise, you will not reach the high notes of sales you seek. When we become adults we get more into our shell and suddenly feel nervous when facing a roomful of people instead singing, out of key notes at the top of our lungs for all the praise at the end. What the hell happened? My humble opinion is that eventually life just beats that fun-loving kid attitude out of you like it was a rented mule. Also, in adulthood the audience isn't as forgiving as it was when you were a kid.

How many uncomfortable presentations have you witnessed? Not just bad presentations, uncomfortable ones where you want to give the presenter a hug and tell the person it will all be OK. In person isn't the only place where stage fright happens. It happens on the phone, in email and negotiations too.

Stage Fright, also known as performance anxiety is when people basically freak out under stressful performance situations. You know, like making that monster pitch in front of the board of directors for a multi-billion dollar company, and freezing like Rick Perry trying to remember three government departments. Words escape you, your knees may feel weak and you could feel dizzy. Seriously, it can debilitate you and ruin your aspirations – hello Perry for President in 2012!

According to Scientific American you also get stage fright because you are such a damn type A perfectionist. Yep, that stuff works against you! Their 2006 article said "...those with performance anxiety are their own harshest critics. They are perfectionists and would rather cancel an appearance — or avoid it — than not meet their own standards and, by extension, not be able to demonstrate how good they are."

So what do perfectionists do? Stick to the script because they are afraid of what will happen if they don't. How do you cope with stage fright? Basically by slowly weaning yourself from the crutches you think you need to perform. The article also points out that an embarrassing performance in grade school can cause you to avoid a similar performance as an adult.[22]

So what do businesses do? Spend millions perpetuating stage fright! The proof is stacked up in storage rooms and piled on the desks of salespeople. They're shiny and make the team feel better — much like a night light in a kid's bedroom, a partition to hide behind or mama's coat tails. Marketers might place these crutches of cold sweats proudly in their portfolio. One-sheets like those can lead to bigger marketing jobs which would be awesome if they also didn't lead to underperforming sales teams.

You might be the proud owner of other scraps of paper that tell you what to say on the phone or what to write in a letter. Usually sales managers type these out once or twice a year to justify their position as well as make sure you — God forbid — don't think for yourself. What are these crispy little creatures? Slicks, scripts and sales sheets.

Sales "slicks" are neat prepackaged "one-sheets" of sales information. If you didn't know, good for you, don't ever become acquainted with them. Slicks are convenient props that encourage salespeople to go for the easy route and not actually think about what a prospect really needs. There are two reasons companies have them: to give marketers something to do, salespeople the path of least resistance to lose a sale and sales managers a prop to show they are guiding the team. Crap, that's three. Crap is a good word actually — it's a synonym for slicks.

When you use a slick you are showing the world that you don't really know squat about your product; worse, have no self-confidence about your sales abilities, or, even worse, want to push your product so you can get a new pair of shoes. In essence, slicks are written scripts you can puke out on a prospect. Problem is one size doesn't fit all and using a slick actually prevents you from becoming more knowledgeable about your product and selling more.

Think back to when you were in second grade and singing in the holiday concert. The music teacher sang the song to you, remember? You learned it by singing, not by reading it off a sheet of paper. In the event the song was written down on paper, your teacher knew you wouldn't be good until the sheet music was gone. Sure, a chorus could sing something off a sheet of paper and get the words and notes right, but to really "feel" the song and give it character the chorus has to get out of the music.

If you never took music class or can't quite remember what it was like, think back to another staple of second-graders: training wheels. Any kid can ride a bike with training wheels, tentatively, wobbling around like a drunk at a DUI stop, upright but not exactly moving in a straight line. Training wheels give kids confidence at first to get out and pedal. But after a while, the wheels become an impediment to true progress. There comes a time to skin a knee and take a fall despite the fear; otherwise kids will never learn to ride. So why do you rely on slicks?

Musicians or actors don't master their performance until the script comes out of the hand — even for the second-grade performers. Glued to the music, a musician never really "feels" the piece and an actor never really plays the part. It takes tossing out that crutch to make real progress. Practicing for the first time without music or a script spotlights strengths and weaknesses in the performance for all the cast to see. Fix those mistakes quickly or the understudy might take your part or the second-grade teacher might pull his hair out. In the end, second-graders can sing and dance without coaching or a sheet of paper to help, and you need a slick to make a sale? Are you kidding me?

Harold Guskin is an accomplished acting coach who has helped Kevin Kline, Peter Fonda, James Gandolfini, Glenn Close and others become better at their craft. In 2003 his book "How to Stop Acting" hit the market. If you need to be convinced that getting away from a script is the way to go, pick up this book and read it. Especially Chapter 1, "Taking It Off the Page."

In this chapter, Guskin discusses his techniques for helping actors truly get a feel for their character, even on the first read of the script. According to Guskin, reading a script turns a creative work into an exercise in analysis and intellect. Actors need to be smart to understand a character, just like salespeople need to be smart to land a deal. Following a script sets an actor on one path and essentially removes the instinct to try new ways of saying the word and truly become the character.

"The actor looks down at the phrase and breathes in and out while he reads the words to himself, giving himself time to let the phrase into his head. Then he looks up from the pages and says the line, no longer reading but speaking. ... As soon as you exhale, say the phrase before you have a chance to censor whatever thought or feeling surfaces. Don't deaden the line by trying to be sincere. Just say what you mean, no matter how startling, stupid, frightening, funny, touching, irreverent, or boring."[23]

This process allows actors to be in a "state of discovery" that leaves them "free to try anything that comes to [them]." That can be scary for some people, and really scary for control freak sales managers or nervous attorneys, which is why sales scripts, sell sheets and letter templates are so prevalent in sales. However, if you are to sell, how are you going to do it if you can't put the product and your belief in that product into your own voice? Just like an actor who can't take it off the page, it's impossible for you to truly be effective in sales if you can't communicate your product, either verbally or written, in your own words.

Doing so requires faith from management and it also requires faith in yourself. You have to be fearless about sounding a little silly and making a few mistakes. You also have to be fearless about taking all the glory and the blame for your sales results.

Making a mistake or two or not knowing your way is all part of the process of feeling what you sell, just like an actor feels a part. Until you lose the script, it won't happen. And as Guskin says, "I would rather find myself throwing away choices because I have too many than have to struggle to find enough colors for the character."

Mark Cuban, the owner of the Dallas Mavericks, appeared on the ABC series "Dancing with the Stars," and yes, I watched an episode or five. What can I say? When Mama is happy, everyone is happy. Anyway, Cuban was paired up with a dancing expert tasked with making him a pro too. Cuban had a problem though — he danced with a pen and pad in hand writing down everything she said. How can you possibly write down a dance?

Cuban's partner thought the same and told him to lose the pad and just feel the dance. She even made him do the steps with his eyes closed. Even a brilliant businessman like Cuban can fall into the trap of using a crutch. Once he tossed it aside, Cuban had his best dance of the season.

Find a top salesperson and ask if that person uses product or sales slicks, scripts or letter guides in any way. You will hear a resounding "NO!" Slicks are the training wheels of sales, the script that gets in the way or the notepad in Mark Cuban's hand. Keep relying on them and you will never truly sell. You won't master your performance because you don't have the guts to simply feel it.

Do yourself a favor. The next time you get in the office, throw all your slicks, scripts and other "guides" away. Don't tell the marketing people because you may hurt their feelings. And don't tell your boss because his power might be threatened. THROW ALL THAT CRAP AWAY! Start responding to clients from the heart, not by tossing some preprinted junk in an envelope.

If you are new to a job, how do you get to the point where you are comfortable? The same way you get to Carnegie Hall — practice, practice, practice. For a phone script, look down and take a breath, look up and read a line, then repeat until you are done. Do it several times a day until you don't have to peek at your script anymore. You will have it memorized by then, right? Far from it. What you should have is your interpretation of the sales script — encompassing cadence, your own feelings and personal experience.

Use the same technique for slicks and letters. Read a line and write it down in your own words. Rinse. Repeat. You will end up with a natural way of relaying the information your company finds so valuable that it will spend thousands of dollars to create nifty sheets and guidelines.

Much like actors connect with the character once they lose the script, what you will find is that your sales will increase because you will start to truly connect with your prospects because you aren't so busy concentrating on the page. You will deliver more tailored solutions and listen more too. All you have to do is crumple up those pieces of paper and make the sales message your own.

Homework:

1) Work through your phone scripts until you discover your own voice and interpretation. Then chuck them.

2) Do the same in written form with all sales slicks and pre-written letters.

Crappy Cold Call: I'm Not a Bother but Still Bothering You

....as you haven't responded to my previous outreach. Please feel free to let me know if you are not interested, I certainly wouldn't want to bother you. (Scold me, then ask me to contact you then say you don't want to bother me. Huh? Oh, that's

right all about your needs and not mine!)

As a reminder, I wanted to inquire about your interest in a brief introduction meeting. My goal is to align with clients who want to grow their business by utilizing a consultative sales model. (Consultative sales model? Not in this email, Champ!)

Without sales there is no business growth, but sales is a discipline that is often ignored and misunderstood. Mindful selling is key to protecting your brand reputation and to acquire clients that are a good fit and will bring you revenue, not a headache. (This paragraph takes the cake. Sales is misunderstood-- especially by this person who isn't even close to mindful selling.)

Our approach is designed to shift the mindset of sales within the organization and make it a fun experience where everybody can contribute and benefit.

Clients chose to work with us because

- They want to fill their pipeline and acquire new clients consistently

- They want to increase revenue

- They want to capture the sales opportunities right under their noses, usually found in existing relationships/clients (Since he doesn't have anything smart to say why not hit em with generic bullet points from a script!)

Those who work with us will build a pipeline, attract more clients and increase their revenue as they develop new business and expand existing relationships. Best of all, this unfettered approach and proven method pays for itself so most organizations that work with us cover their investment by attracting new clients in a short period of time. (A product that pays for itself? What an original compelling argument-NOT! I've found that some of the worst sales communications come from sales training companies. Really makes you want to use them, doesn't it?)

Feel free to visit our website at [Website] or simply reply to this e-mail and we can set-up a time for you to learn more. (Clearly he's clueless about selling so why not follow up for him, too?)

Warm wishes,

[Salesperson]

Cool Cold Call: A Good Sales Services Email

Dear Chad,

Please forgive my cold email introduction, but if increasing sales effectiveness is at the top of your agenda, we suggest that you take a look at our white paper on Guided Buying and Selling. (Rather than puking "I" all over me this guy quickly gets to how he can help me. And he offers something useful all in one sentence! Eureka!)

This is all about extending your Salesforce.com platform with tools that better guide your sales people – directly at the point of customer interaction – to measurably increase sales effectiveness and reduce pilot error at critical stages of the buying and selling cycle.

I should be delighted to set-up an online meeting to explore this further with you. (Dude! Who cares if you will be delighted?

How about "in five minutes you will be convinced this is the way to go. I will call you at X time.)

Best regards,

[Salesperson]

Grade: B-. Points off for the whole "forgive my email introduction" because he could care less and for the lame close.

Lesson 6: Social Studies — Your Personal Simon Cowell

//

"So few people are truly themselves when they're in the spotlight."

— Lucinda Williams, singer-songwriter

It's bound to happen. You are going to have to go out with clients and prospects to an event or dinner or some kind of function. Time for you to be "on" no matter how badly you would rather be with your loved ones. That's business, right?

Business functions can either be sheer torture or pretty fun, but most of the time something in between. Exactly how should you act? Professional or like yourself or should you have your "game face" on? Most people put on the business personality when they are in social business settings, or worse, in the office. Come on, don't you act differently in a business setting than with friends? Why not act like you would if you were just slugging a few beers and watching the game? Imagine how killer it would be to not have to work so hard at work?

Fear not, my friend, you aren't alone; lots of people put on a "game face" when at the office or out with clients. People assume others notice everything they do and say and lock those actions up in a vast mental checklist. It's called the "spotlight effect."

Oh, man, everyone is staring at you! Don't make a mistake now, because people will mark it down like a judge on "Dancing with the Stars." Just like that dancing show, the notion that we are always judged is prevalent in mass media. Check out all the programs that have a panel of judges, blogs on the Internet, gossip columns or, gasp, your annual review! Seems everyone has his or her own personal Simon Cowell. No wonder people feel the harsh glow of the spotlight and as a result act like they think people want them to act. Which, as you will read, crushes your productivity and thus your sales.

Unless you are a contestant on the world's greatest dancer-singer-illusionist-trivia buff-fashion designer show, people notice much less than you think. As for your annual review, do you think your boss could justify his position by focusing on all the great stuff you did? Heck, no! Training the spotlight on things you "need to improve on" makes for a meaty annual review to prove how hard your boss is working. Reviews are part of the circle of life's bullshit and you shouldn't let them change who you are and how you act.

According to a Journal of Personality and Social Psychology article, the spotlight effect is when "people tend to believe the social spotlight shines more brightly on them than it really does." Part of that belief is "native realism," which is the "common tendency to assume that one's perception of an object or event is an accurate reflection of its objective properties, not a subjective interpretation." Guess what? It's very subjective. Top that off with the "they're out to get me" special — "self-as-target bias."

This is the "sense that actions or events are disproportionately directed toward the self" or you. Ever felt in a meeting like a general comment by your boss was somehow directed just at you? That's it. Or if you forgot some of your presentation materials and just know the prospect was going to ask you about it. Just call yourself "target boy" because people don't recognize you or direct their actions toward you as much as you think.

To prove the spotlight effect, professors Thomas Gilovich of Cornell University, Victoria Husted Medvec of Northwestern University and Kenneth Savitsky of Williams College messed with lots of students. Seriously, with the support of grants from the National Science Foundation, the professors conducted four scientific experiments with student participants.

Without knowledge of what was actually being tested, Cornell

University students were asked to wear a T-shirt with a big picture of Barry Manilow on the front. Since college students wouldn't be caught dead listening to the guy who makes "the whole world sing," the professors theorized those students would be embarrassed to wear the shirt. Interviews proved the professors were correct — the students who had to wear the Barry Manilow shirts (participants) indeed felt like assuming the fetal position under a table.

Would people notice such embarrassment? Six classrooms held other students (observers) sitting on one side of a long table each filling out a questionnaire. They were overseen by an "instructor." One of the participants wearing the Manilow T-shirt knocked on the door, entered the room and was instructed to sit opposite the observers filling out the questionnaire. But just when the participant was about to sit the instructor sent the student back out of the room. So you have an interruption, close contact (face to face across a table) and then exit between the participant and the observers.

The participants were asked, "How many of the people in the room you were just in would be able to tell me who is on your T-shirt?" Then the observers were individually asked if they noticed who was on the shirt. To confirm the results and put to rest notions of weak powers of observation, control groups watched videotapes of the experiments and weighed in as well.

Nearly 50 percent of the participants thought Barry Manilow was noticed. Only 25 percent of the observers actually did notice. Yep, the spotlight effect was shining brightly. "The average estimate made by the targets was exactly twice as high as the average accuracy rate of the observers." Because the estimates of the participants exceeded that of the control group it indicated "the feeling of being in the spotlight, not faulty abstract theories about the salience of T-shirt images or the powers of observation of the typical observer." Again, participant T-shirts were noticed only half as much as the participants thought they would be.

Wearing the T-shirt of someone you think is a dork might make you act embarrassed, especially if you are forced to wear it by an evil professor using you to get published. The professors considered the same notion so they conducted a second experiment. This time, new participants got to choose from three T-shirts of famous people the participants would feel "good about wearing."

Then, just like in experiment one, participants interrupted more students filling out a questionnaire. Since the new participants felt good about wearing the new T-shirt, they wouldn't act embarrassed. Again, control groups were used to help verify results.

With the embarrassment removed, surely the participants wouldn't overestimate who noticed their T-shirt. NOT! On average the participant's estimate was six times higher than the observers. Six times higher, and the participants were proud to wear the shirt! A large majority of people really didn't notice. What does that say about how much people absorb when you are making a sales pitch about a wonderful product for which you believe? We'll talk about that later. Back to hapless student manipulation!

Most people don't notice what you wear, good or bad — the professors proved that in experiments one and two. That must be because people are so engrossed in the things you have to say, good or bad, that the only thing they notice is your dazzling display of verbal intellect, right? Seems reasonable. As one of my salespeople used to say, "Chad is wonderful. If you don't believe him, just ask him!" You're in sales so you must have a healthy ego too. People hang on your every word too, I'm sure.

The professors wondered, do people think their actions, both positive and negative stand out "more to others than they actually do?" Groups of three to seven students were asked to talk about the problem of inner cities as if they were on a committee tasked with addressing the issue. After 20 minutes of discussion, the participants would spend 10 minutes creating a joint "policy statement" recommending their solution.

Once this was complete the participants were split up to separately answer a series of questions about the exercise. Four questions asked participants "to estimate how the group as a whole (on average) would rank all of the group members, themselves included, in terms of: (a) how much they advanced the discussion, (b) the number of speech errors they made, (c) the number of comments they made that may have offended someone, and (d) the number of comments they made that other members of the group might judge critically." Once that was done, each participant was asked the same questions again "from their own perspective — as they themselves saw things." The difference between "how participants thought others would rank them and how everyone else actually did rank them" would determine if the spotlight effect was at play or not.

To add wattage to the spotlight (or not) participants were also asked how much time each participant spent talking during the discussion. They were also asked to rank the top five most "remarkable comments" made, be they positive or negative remarks. To help with this task, the participants were given seating charts to remind them of the large name tags each participant wore.

You don't want to read all the t statistics and p values of the calculations between what participants thought compared to what the group thought, do you? Good, that math makes my head spin too. Bottom line is this: Individual participants significantly overestimated how high the other group members would rank them in advancing the discussion, speech errors, offensive comments, comments judged critically, remarkable comments and percentage of time spent talking.

Take it from the professors: "Whether assessing their positive or negative contributions, participants overestimated the salience of their own behavior to the other members of the group. They thought that the other group members would rank them significantly higher on all six dimensions than the other group members actually did. It thus appears that the average person's actions command less attention from others than he or she suspects, and that the social spotlight may shine less brightly than he or she believes."

Man ... guess I'm not so special and noticed after all. Sorry, neither are you. Depending on the situation, this can be a good thing or a bad thing. We'll talk about it after experiment four in which it's proved that, more than we ever let on, we think we are wonderful and that people notice us.

Students, it's time to introduce you to the final piece of the spotlight effect: anchoring-and-adjustment. This means that people can be so focused on the appropriateness of their own behavior in a given situation that they find it difficult to "escape the anchor of their own experience when estimating how their actions appear to others." In non-psychobabble speak it means we all have a deeply personal perspective on how things should go in the world.

This type of "egocentrism," or focusing on our own view of the ways of the world, is strongest in — you guessed it — young children. Second-graders, anyone? And guess what? Even though it isn't as strong when you are an adult, it significantly influences the way you view a given situation.

People check with their internal set of values and experience to evaluate how they think other people expect them to act in a given situation, or how people judged them in a given situation. "But, as is typically the case with such processes, the adjustment or correction tends to be insufficient, and so estimates of how one appears to others are overly influenced by how one appears to oneself." How did the professors find out how participants arrived at their answers? Simple. The professors asked.

It's difficult for people to accurately describe mental processes, so the professors didn't expect a detailed explanation about how participants came to their conclusions. What the professors were looking for was an answer to a specific question: "Had [participant] considered any responses other than the one they first gave?"

Conducting T-shirt test No. 1 again, the professors asked the participants (students who wore the embarrassing T-shirt) how many observers could identify the embarrassing person (in this case rapper Vanilla Ice) on the shirt. Then the professors asked if participants had considered a different answer before they gave the final one.

Just like the other experiments, the participants grossly overestimated how many people would notice Vanilla Ice Ice Baby on their T-shirt. As for if they changed their answer, 73 percent did and all of them started with a higher estimate than what they ultimately conveyed. This supports the contention that people realize they are estimating another's response based on personal "life experience" and know that's not the way all people think. Acknowledging that realization, we "adjust" our expectations about how much others notice what we do or the way we appear. Problem is that adjustment is never strong enough and we still overestimate the impact of our words and appearance.

Wow. That's cool. And ... so?

So? Are you kidding? This has enormous sales implications! The next chapter explains them. But first a little bit of homework.

Homework:

1) In your next internal meeting try real hard to remember what people were wearing. An hour later jot down the names and description of what they wore. Check during the day to see how many you get right.

2) After your next five sales calls, for a fun follow-up email your prospect the next day to ask them what five things they remember from your pitch. Tell them its an experiment or part of your training. Come to think of it, this might be a good idea for follow-up after all your sales calls.

Crappy Cold Call: Shit on the Wall

Chad,

Sorry for the Monday interruption, I did try and call but unfortunately had no luck. I'm just looking for some guidance on who I should speak with in your organization. (How can you be sorry if in the next breath you are asking me to help you and explaining how you can help me?)

We are an agency support group existing solely to help agencies like yours serve their clients with gift cards as promotional gifts. Touted as today's most effective incentive, our participating gift card partners are second to none (Ready. Fire. Aim! Funny how everyone says they are "best in class" but few can actually show it.) *and include Visa, Wal-Mart, Exxon Mobil, Panera Bread, Target, Best Buy, Kohl's and around 100 others.* (In other words: "Since I don't have anything smart, relevant or strategic to say, why don't we play show and tell?" The tell-tale sign of a poor salesperson is reaching for the product before a need is recognized or revealed.) *These consumer facing promotions are easy to implement, the program is turnkey, licensing and signage are included, the gift cards are discounted and we exist behind the scenes to help your agency bring best-in-class promotions to your clients should they have a need for a mainstream and popular promotional gift.*

I'm more than happy to send you a few visual examples of what some other agencies have done so please just say the word and I'll do it. (Instead of spending 30 seconds to get a clue on what our company actually does, just sling the "current client list" shit against the wall? Maybe it will stick!)

Have a great day,
[Salesperson]

Lesson 7: Spring Play — Ways to Turn Off the Spotlight

//

Gotta get myself some cheap sunglasses.
— ZZ Top

You go into a sales meeting ready to slay them. Why wouldn't you? Compared to all the other salespeople you saw at the convention, you rock! Besides you just got a new suit and a new haircut. What's not to like? Add your company's brand new logo mug and the deal is yours.

You meet and the prospect is agreeing with everything you say! She is eating out of your hand, nodding like crazy, smiling and gently stroking your product. She even checked out your hair and new suit and listened attentively when you made small talk about the picture of her kids on the desk.

The prospect says she loves you and wants to "take the next step." You send her some follow-up information and call to set up a follow-up appointment with her boss. Of course you would like to make it then but she has to check her boss' schedule. You agree to "chat next week" and leave your card.

Yes! Another great sales meeting. She was excited and you couldn't have been better. This one is in the bag! Which of course you would know isn't the case if you employed the RoseClose, but you can still be excited, right?

Next week rolls around and you can't get her on the phone. What the hell? Didn't she say she wanted some more info and to move forward? A week later, your obviously distracted prospect finally picks up the phone. Yep, she got the stuff you sent, white envelope with a red product folder and some slicks inside (no! not slicks!). Give her another week, she is checking it out.

That's OK, you guess. Except for one problem — you use green envelopes and your product folder is yellow and because you're smart, you didn't use any Godforsaken slicks! She has *no clue* who you are. Worse, she thinks you are a competitor! How did that happen!

Question: When you were in your wonderful first meeting, did you feel warm? You should have because the spotlight effect was glaring down on you. Pack the SPF on your next sales call and grab some cheap sunglasses because you are going to get burned!

You were nothing but part of the intellectual blur of your prospect's very busy life and you must work hard at shutting down the spotlight effect to increase your sales. Look in the mirror and ask yourself: "How do I and the products I sell stand out from the crowd?" Write down your answer, then stick it on a copy machine and reduce it by 83 percent. Because as you know from reading the experiments in the previous chapter, when wearing a shirt they were proud of, participants said recognition was *six times* higher than actual.

I'd argue it's even worse for us "if you don't believe he's wonderful just ask him" salespeople. Ego is great when you need to accept rejection. But when it comes to separating you from the pack, it's your worst enemy. You don't stand out from the crowd anywhere near as much as you think.

When I was writing this chapter I went to a sales meeting at a major health system on the East Coast. As I walked toward the glass office doors some other guys in suits came along because they had a meeting too. Just then the person they were meeting with came around the corner, looked at all of us, me included, and said, "Oh, you're from company X." I replied, "Nope, not me, just them," and he still addressed me like I was.

Hello? Dude, I'm not with them! To him, I was just another guy in a suit making a sales call despite the fact that I told him I wasn't with that company. Must have been a lot on his mind because he didn't catch it. It couldn't have been that I looked like just another suit. No way! I stand out. Gimme my sunglasses. Shit!

How many impressive guy or gals, *like you*, do you think prospects see every day? How busy do you think they are? And we think we are six times more memorable than we actually are. Chances are that's conservative for salespeople. I bet we overestimate how much prospects absorb and differentiate us by *10* times.

How could we not notice such a gulf in perception? Great salespeople, like you, even just good ones, train themselves to notice subtle verbal and physical cues. Since most of the time we aren't getting the full story from prospects, we try to read the underlying meaning in what a prospect says and determine when we have hit a "hot button" simply by body language or other cues.

Kind of like a snake charmer with a cobra, you can actually see a prospect sit up when you finally hit the point that will actually make the person buy. Salespeople intuitively read other people in a sales meeting and should constantly work on impressive observation, like I'm sure you do.

Problem is you are meeting with people who are not professional salespeople. The folks you sell to could be marketers, CEOs, VPs, regular people or (gag) purchasing agents. You get the picture, people not schooled in observing and remembering subtle cues and verbal signals. It only makes sense that someone accustomed to rapt concentration in meetings would assume everyone else is doing the same. After all, you are human and all of us use anchoring-and-adjustment to evaluate social situations. But in reality, people aren't noticing that much at all.

When it comes to meetings and presentations, you have done your homework and prepared intelligent questions specifically for your prospects — not boneheaded ones like, "So tell me what you do?" You have great examples of how you have helped clients just like them, and know the background of your main contact. This is step one in separating you from the pack — most salespeople simply don't make the extra effort.

I know this for sure because I have had the pleasure (or displeasure) of interviewing hundreds of "salespeople" for open positions at McMurry. McMurry is one of the best places to work in America, so it's tough for applicants to even get through the door. You would think that once an applicant does, they would be as prepared as can be.

Sadly that is not the case, even with people wishing to secure a sales position. And if you can't be prepared when you are selling yourself — trying to feed your family, get the money to buy a car, pay off loans or all of the above — how prepared are you going to be in "just" a sales call? Not very.

If I were to guess how many job candidates came through the door knowing information about McMurry not found on our website, information about me that can be discovered with a simple Google search, and intelligently prepared questions and ideas of how to innovate in the job for which they are interviewing — basic preparation as far as I'm concerned — it would be one out of 100.

So, step one in getting people to take notice: Be more prepared for a sales meeting than you ever imagined necessary, every time. Doing so instantly makes you one in 100. Yes it takes extra work. But instead of frittering your life away watching TV or surfing the Net or trying to hit some stupid number of phone calls in a day goal, wouldn't you rather make money? To make sure my sales team does this, we employ strategy from the book "Flawless Execution" by James D. Murphy. This book applies to business the steps fighter pilots use to prepare for battle. It works. Read it and apply it.

Step two: Become a servant. My dad was an unbelievable oil salesman. Sure it had something to do with being affable and asking for a sale. But when I look back at his career what stands out is how he served both his prospects and his customers. From a business standpoint he would serve them by first showing up with a very good idea of the challenges a car dealership was facing, knowledge of the key players in the account and a solution for them.

And then he would just show up and give. Give till it hurts. Talk about solutions and give his knowledge to the prospect in the first meeting. There was no holding back, he was there to serve. It didn't take long before prospects started to realize that Dad genuinely wanted to help them. The question of buying was out of the question. Instead, it was a foregone conclusion.

His prospects had to have the solution because they knew it would help them solve their problems and/or make more money. It was about the prospect, not him. There was no second-grade selling to be had when he made a pitch. He was one of the top salespeople in the company because of it. When you truly give, without expectation of something in return, it's amazing what you get back.

And if you cry about selling in a "commodity market," suck that lower lip in and dab your eyes once and for all. Stop making excuses. Kill that self-fulfilling prophecy. Motor oil. You don't get much more commodity than that. And his oil was the highest priced. Yes, it had special additives and came in a yellow bottle, but boil it down and it was oil. Servant selling helped get the job done.

This type of selling is "putting the furniture in the house." If you have ever shopped for a home or apartment or sell them, then you know what I'm talking about. When you walk into a home and start talking about where you will put the furniture — the couch over here, that special picture over there, painting the wall a certain color, then you are emotionally buying into that vision. Suddenly you can afford a little more. You ask your agent questions, talk about making an offer. It's not a matter of if you will buy it, it's when and the sooner the better. That is putting the furniture in the house. It's the point in the sales pitch in which you just sit back and let your prospects do the talking because they envision how your solution will help them.

No matter what you sell, you can do it.

And once a prospect became a client, my dad gave even more. He made them raving fans who told other people they would be crazy not to buy from him. One of his best tools was his Pennzoil Grill Team. Car dealers usually have staffs of 100 or more and vendors streaming in and out all day long. How many do you think show up with grills, tables, hamburgers, hot dogs, homemade baked beans, coleslaw, potato salad and all the fixins? How many of those vendors do you think do it on their day off? And how many do you think stand there in front of a hot grill in the Florida sun, cook the burgers and dogs, serve them to every employee — including the owners — and say thanks for using their product? ONE. My dad.

What started off as a couple of gas grills eventually turned into a Pennzoil Grill Team trailer painted by a car dealer at cost, custom grill and stellar reputation. Think my dad stood out from everyone asking car dealers to buy something? As sure as cheese on a burger he did. No spotlight effect for him. He was 10 times as smart, creative and hardworking as his competitors and he wasn't even paid commission! If you're paid commission and you aren't doing things like this, what the hell's the matter with you?

Becoming memorable takes hard work. And with hard work come the rewards.

Three: Break on through to the other side — do original things. Ever seen a prospect laugh during one of your presentations? Not a polite chuckle. We're talking sidesplitting, knee-slapping laughter — letting go with glee. Back in the "old days" of selling, meetings would start with a joke, just to lighten the mood. Man, how contrived. And who knows what people will think is appropriate or not, especially these days when it seems like nothing is appropriate anymore.

Still, those old-timers knew what to do. Laughter lowers defenses and done right makes people like you. It allows you to break on through from the business to the personal side. But now you have to be much more skilled and genuine to make it happen. Now you have to create laughter simply by being yourself and having fun. One of the best ways is to make fun of yourself Have some cajones and be edgy. Take a calculated risk. Don't be an idiot, but every now and then a little edge can break the ice. If you have done your homework, you may have enough knowledge to razz them about their favorite sports team. You know, be a *real person* not a *salesperson.*

Caution, every now and then this will blow up in your face! There are some truly boring ass people in this world with miserable lives and misery loves company. And they hate happy fun people like you. But the majority will think it's refreshing to meet someone with a personality. Just try to keep it clean, at least in the first meeting.

From time to time, we will take pictures during our road trips to break the boredom, and make presentations to the rest of our company about what life is really like on the road. And if you are a non-salesperson reading this, then let's be clear about one thing: There is very little glamour in a sales trip.

One day we were visiting with some VPs in Connecticut. The meeting went as planned and we were tying them down for the follow-up. Then we made one more request. "Hey, would you mind posing for a picture for us? Could you act like we are twisting your arm and forcing you to sign a contract?" Our prospect agreed and we took the picture.

As a follow-up to our meeting, we sent a copy of the shot to our prospect with a note saying, "Don't make us have to do this again!" A 42-cent stamp, a note and a little effort separated us from the pack. Our prospect loved the humor and put the picture on his bulletin board. We made things fun and in the process took the elephant out of the room — sign the contract. And you know what? He eventually did.

When a prospect has a cold, we overnight herbal tea in one of our mugs. Yes, we have logo mugs but only use them when there will be impact. If someone has a baby or announces a pregnancy, we send a handmade baby blanket. Hear about vacation plans? We'll send a book on the destination or better yet some "insider" advice from an employee who has been there. As a rule of thumb, if you would do it for a good friend, you should do it for the prospect. Even more for a prospect because they pay you, friends don't! It doesn't have to be expensive, just thoughtful. And that leads to ...

Four: Be a person. Sure having fun will help separate you from the pack and so will small personal touches, but it will also show another part of you. The human part. Instantly you aren't just a salesman trying to push a product. Instead you are a person trying to help.

How many times do you ask, or are you asked, "How are you doing?" Saying, "How are you doing?" is one of those things pounded into your head by the time you're a second-grader.

"How are you?"

"Fine."

"How are you doing?"

"Fine."

"How's (insert city)?"

"Fine."

Since every salesperson on earth asks this question right out of the gate, why don't you say something different that makes you a person and separates you from the pack? Something like, "Did you know you come up No. 4 when I Google your name?" or "What are you doing answering the phone? Do you know how much snow you are getting? If I lived there I would be out snowboarding." Or "I just read about your new product launch and thought of you."

And when they ask how you are, why do you blow such a golden opportunity by saying, "fine"? They are asking about you! You now have permission to talk just about you. The rest of the meeting should be 100 percent focused on the needs of your prospect. But right now you have slow pitch to show you are a person!

Why would you say "good" or "fine" or "great"? Why not, "Couldn't be better, this morning my son said his first words." Or "You know I didn't get busted speeding alone in the HOV lane this morning so life is good!" Or "Motivated enough to actually get some exercise in this morning." Or "Great, after all they booted that loser on 'Dancing with the Stars.'" Or my personal favorite: "Kick ass! Happy hour is in just one hour, 52 minutes and 33 seconds!"

Answering "fine" makes you a robot. Saying something quickly about yourself, even quirky, makes you a living, breathing person. One of the things my kids get the most excited about in school is show and tell. Time to say or show something cool just about them. The other second-graders giggle and get to know their classmates a little more.

Being all business in a sales situation is sure to typecast you like all those other sales robots. Saying "fine" is also a clear indication you are rushing to why you called and what you want to say. Lay back a little. Relax. Take that gift. Give them a good answer.

Sure there's risk involved in this. Every now and then you will get some stiff who never liked show and tell. But more times than not, people on the other line or across the desk are dying to have fun. They are *working after all*. And how fun is that?

Five: Make your competitors bitch. This is one of my measures of success — how much competitors bitch about us. I love to make them squirm by outsmarting them. When we hear, "Well, you know, some vendors weren't happy with how much noise you guys were making at the convention and complained," we high-five. You know why? Because we beat competitor asses and they know it.

What's better? Competitors specifically naming your company in a competitive presentation. Something along the lines of, "Unlike company A, we give complete customization." Oh really? If you were a prospect and you heard that, wouldn't you run right to the phone and call company A? Yep, and that's what happens. Our direct competitors hate us. Cool.

It's not because we're nasty to them; in fact we go out of our way to smile and say hello to competitors at trade shows. Better yet, march into their booth and shake hands. You should hear nervous laughter because you consistently outsmart, out-hustle and outwork them. The competitors bitch because they feel better blaming others rather than themselves.

I'm all for karma but if it's between hitting sales goals and remodeling your kitchen or sending your kids to college, are you going to let up on your competitors for a second? Didn't think so. Want to consistently bury them? Make improvement and differentiation a constant. You will know your competitors are beaten if they start bitching.

If they complain about noise at a trade show, next year use lights. If they complain about lights, have a cook serving them their lunch the year after. If they complain about the smell, hold an event with the talent in your company as the entertainment. When competitors start crying, you are in their head. You know, they will be asking, "I wonder what company A is going to pull out this year?" ratherhan focusing on their own strategy to win. Get it? Before your competitors have even thought of what to bitch about, you should know how to juke them next year.

When competitors start crying, "That isn't fair! Company A shouldn't be able to do that!" — then they may start reacting to and changing the way they present both their company and themselves. Pretty soon, they don't really know what to say. It's much like a politician being knocked "off message" by his opponent. As you will read in the next chapter, trying to present yourself differently can really destroy your mojo.

Homework:

1) Write down 10 responses to the question "how are you?" Use them instead of answering "fine."

2) Think of 10 more engaging things you can ask prospects other than "how are you?"

Crappy Cold Call: Homework Anyone?

I'd like to arrange a time to speak with you and others within your organization regarding mobile applications. (Me and "others?" So, would the janitor be okay?) *My company, is a premier provider of B2B, B2C and B2E mobile apps. We create high-impact mobile apps for the iPhone, iPad, Android and BlackBerry devices. Our apps deliver an extremely high ROI.*

We've created hundreds of enterprise level mobile apps for the Global 500. Our development team is 100% in house. They consist of some of the brightest and most accomplished mobile engineers in the world. I urge you to get to know our team - their education, expertise and market experience – [Website]. Let us know which team members you feel would be best for your program. (Well, with that huge list and the self-proclaimed expertise why wouldn't I give you all the relevant team members?)

Our prototype mockup and mobile consulting service is $9,500 and takes about a month to complete. (Slow down! We just met and you are already talking money?) *The app can be delivered within an additional sixty days - thus start to finish is generally ninety days. Attached to this letter is a PDF that describes our prototype, consulting, PoC and development process. The PDF also lists roughly*

30 functions provided by our code library. (Why not say something relevant instead of another list? Homework anyone? Come to think of it had she done her homework she never would have sent this. We sell apps too!) *I've asked my executive assistant, [name], to give you a telephone call to arrange a time to speak.* (I thought she was so important and slammed that her executive assistant was going to call? They never did.)

Let me know the DATE and TIME you are available for this conference call and web-ex style presentation. You can also immediately and directly reserve a time on my calender via this link – [Web address]. I look forward to speaking with you soon.

Sincerely,
[Name]
Vice President of Business Development

Lesson 8: Physical Education — Zonked Out and Drooling

//

The word aerobics came about when the gym instructors got together and said, "If we're going to charge $10 an hour, we can't call it jumping up and down."

— Rita Rudner

Of course you get some exercise, hit the weights, run or walk, rollerblade, do something physical. Then you know there's only so much physical activity you can take before you are shot. Plum tuckered. Worn out. What about mental tasks? Working on a project or a hard report hour after hour can really wear you down till eventually the words swim and you start making mistakes.

Second-graders charge hard too, all day. Whether its kickball, kicking around subtraction or music class, they go all out. And if you have ever hung around one, then you know when a second-grader runs out of juice: He gets irrational, cranky, cries uncontrollably — you know kind of like a salesperson losing a big deal. There just isn't anything left in the tank to fuel them until suddenly the second-grader is zonked out and drooling in the back seat of the car on the way home.

Did you know you have different batteries in your body? You could be mentally exhausted but have the energy to go out and run a couple of miles, or vice versa. Mental and physical energy, that's all there is, right?

Not so fast, buddy! Researchers think they have nailed down another fuel tank in your body — the fuel cell you use to regulate the way you act. But this fuel tank is much smaller and when the charge runs out you could be babbling like a second-grader.

Perhaps you have seen the new "electric hybrid" cars manufacturers are developing. General Motors arguably had a big head start with its "Chevy Volt." The Volt is designed to run 25-50 miles on just the battery power you get from plugging the car in at night like a cellphone. When that runs out, a small engine kicks in to recharge batteries about 30 percent while you are driving and gets 344 miles with just over 9 gallons of gas.

If only the human body worked so well with its various fuel sources. Problem is the fuel tank that supplies energy for you to present yourself favorably to others is pretty small. "Self's resources" are the energy that fuels what psychologists call "self-presentation."

Self-presentation is what we "turn on" when we make a business presentation, meet new people or are in unfamiliar or difficult social situations. We use it to be the most professional — on our best behavior — and present ourselves the way we think people expect us to. Are you thinking really hard about what you say before you say it? You are self-presenting. Are you acutely aware of being professional, sitting up straight or presenting yourself "in the best light"? You are tapping into your self's resources reservoir.

Tax the battery too much though and it will negatively affect everything else you are trying to accomplish — like appear knowledgeable in a sales pitch. And like a second-grader, if you wear yourself out, it could affect your ability to concentrate, control emotions and master performances.[24]

Self-presentation has bit you in the ass, guaranteed. For those of you who are married or in serious relationships, do you remember the first time you met your partner's parents? Not your best day, was it? You were trying to be on your best behavior, project what you thought the 'rents wanted to see and what happened? Things probably went good for the first few hours — you were on your best behavior, presenting the way you thought they expected, but as the clocked ticked on you wilted under the heat of scrutiny. In the end I bet you said or did something so damn embarrassing they still talk about to this day.

Countless movies have been made around this very theme: "Meet the Parents" with Ben Stiller, for example, in which he does well at first, then manages to break his future sister-in-law's nose, lose the cat and catch the yard on fire (just for starters) as a result of his effort to impress the family. Draining the self's resources can lead to mondo mistakes.

Goodness knows I've done it. Seems as if every time my wife tells me not to say something in a social situation I say something worse! Just trying too hard, I guess. Works for most of the night and until the tank gets low and I blow it. What's difficult about her requests (sorry, honey) is that most of the time they are counter to my normal behavior.

I'm a confident, energetic, delightfully witty, sarcastic, opinionated and driven individual and that's the way it is, baby! If you don't believe it, just ask me! Some might say a more accurate description is cocky, obnoxious, boisterous, crude and brash with just two "verbal filter" settings: low and off. What the hell do they know?

While I've worked very hard at smoothing the rough edges of my wonderfully dynamic personality, I am who I am and I gotta be me. Because you know what? When I try hard to be someone else and "not screw up" guess what I do? Screw up worse.

It's no wonder we have to work so hard at "being something." Truth is all of us are damned confused. We're faced with tons of choices using a brain not too evolved from hunter-gatherer tribes from thousands of years ago. So grunt, grab a stick and chase your cat around the house because you aren't too far removed and besides, what else are cats good for besides making rank litter boxes?

Don't think you're that close to the spear-throwing cousins of yesteryear? Really? Because unless you're a book-skimming CEO, you should know from actually reading this book that there's gonna be science to back it up. Better, controversial science written more than 30 years ago that still has some camps in a lather.

Edward O. Wilson is a brilliant Harvard professor and scientist who introduced sociobiology in 1977. According to Wilson, sociobiology is the "scientific study of the biological basis of all forms of social behavior in all kinds of organisms, including man." In a nutshell, it means our societies aren't too far removed from those of insects, monkeys and other animals; that genetics drives much of what we do; and that monkey and insect cultures are pretty darn close to us. Feel free to freak out over this or nod in agreement.

Regardless of your personal stand on sociobiology, Wilson does bring up a good point: that we are animals wired for a simple existence living in a world with complex decisions. Basically we have hunter-gatherer genes with the demands of modern society placed upon them.

"Where the hunter-gatherer fills at most one or two informal roles out of only several available, his literate counterpart in an industrial society must choose 10 or more out of thousands, and replace one set with another at different periods of his life or even at different times of the day. Futhermore, each occupation ... is played just so, regardless of the true workings of the mind behind the persona. ... Daily life is a compromised blend of posturing for the sake of role-playing and of varying degrees of self-revelation. Under these stressful conditions even the 'true' self cannot be precisely defined."[25]

So, if you feel frustrated at work or feel like you aren't being your "true self," you can blame it on those dudes who scribbled petroglyphs on cave walls. You have their genes. Even so, modern society, especially business, requires us to behave in a manner more refined than slaying buffalo. This takes a ton of effort. More than you may think, which brings us back to the self-preservation fuel cell residing in all of us.

Not to make you too much of my own personal Dr. Phil, but a few years ago I had a problem. Every now and then when particularly stressed out in business situations, I would just blow my top and become an irrational drooling freak. In an effort to fix the silly behavior akin to a second-grader who didn't get breakfast, or a hunter-gatherer confused by too many choices, my ever patient and loving boss Fred finally told me to knock it off once and for all.

Like a good addict trying to kick a habit, I counted off the days without a blowup. One. Five. Seventeen. Twenty-seven. Really worked on my demeanor at work, even changed the way I dressed to appear more professional and "together," only to come home exhausted, demoralized and confused. What a sad sack.

Look, treating everyone with respect 100 percent of the time was not only a reasonable request, it's just the right thing to do — and Fred had every right to demand it of me. Problem was trying to put on a "work face" drained my self-presentation tank to the point where I made more mistakes and had a crappy sales year to boot. It was damn near impossible to tiptoe around and second-guess myself. Eventually I learned I could be me and be respectful all the time no matter the level of stress, which was much easier than putting on a perceived persona. Thank you, my personal Dr. Phil, I feel better now.

What kind of persona are you trying to put on? Or are you being yourself? It's an important and vital question because you will exhaust yourself and make more mistakes if you act like someone you aren't.

Kathleen Vohs, Carlson School of Management, University of Minnesota, has a doctorate in psychological and brain sciences and specializes in areas including self-regulation. Roy Baumeister, The Florida State University (GO NOLES!), has a doctorate in psychology and specializes in areas including self-presentation. The two co-wrote an article for the Journal of Personality and Social Psychology that says, "Some evidence suggests that the same [self's] resource is used for widely different self-regulatory tasks, including regulation of cognition and thought, of emotion, of impulsive and appetitive behaviors and performances. Accordingly, the limited resource model predicts that if a person attempts to engage in several demanding self-regulatory tasks simultaneously or consecutively, the chance of success at any one of them is significantly reduced."

Let's face it, when you're in a sales situation, you're dealing with cognition (psychology speak for thinking, learning and judging) and performance; two things tapping your limited self's resource. Layer on a serving of putting on a persona and you're looking at No. 3. Skip breakfast, stay up late or party like Lindsey Lohan before reporting to the morgue for community service and you toss in appetitive behavior — in this case thinking about satisfying a need like one of those yummy free cinnamon rolls at a Holiday Inn, needing sleep or a big old bottle of Gatorade.

The deck is stacked against you. The big question is: Why the hell do you do it? Bigger question: Do you expect to do well in a sales presentation when all of that other stuff is vying for your precious self-presentation resource?

Ever seen a juggler add more balls to the act? The more in the air, the tougher it is to juggle. So goes it with your self-presentation. You want to reduce the number of balls you have in the air to just one: focusing on your prospect.

Get ready to say, "Well, duh!" If you want to present at your best, you must eat well, get a good night's sleep and not slam drinks like a frat boy. (Well, duh!) Here's the problem though: Many people don't do that, and my guess is you've been guilty a time or two.

How many times have you pushed it by checking into the hotel late, getting up early and skipping breakfast before the big meeting? It's a well-known fact that second-graders and all kids for that matter do better in school when they have a good breakfast and better nutrition. So why do we give it up as adults?

Too busy isn't an excuse, either. You make time for what you want to do. Not surprisingly, Baumeister talks about glucose levels as being key to your self-presentation prowess. The lower your blood sugar the bigger risk of dropping balls, and no caffeine isn't a suitable substitute.

Pile limited self resources on top of not controlling variables, wishful thinking, self-fulfilling prophecies, the spotlight effect, and following scripts and you can see why you're missing your numbers. So to help alleviate that issue, your boss drops big bucks to attend the big convention. And that's when things get even worse.

Homework:

Create a business trip and meeting check list. Detail how much you are going to exercise, sleep, meals you are going to eat, things to avoid (booze) and the steps you are going to take during each trip and before each meeting. Check it off. Use it to keep all your fuel tanks as full as possible.

Crappy Cold Call: The Shotgun

Hi,

Please pass this email who is in charge of sales or marketing in your company. (Um, I can send a generic, poorly written shotgun email to nameless people pretty easily, don't you think?)

Companies have budget to spend before end of this quarter.

Purchasing an email list for your sales and marketing would be a good idea but what if it won't serve a purpose intended for? (This is a benefit to me...I think.)

I have two options open for you

1) I will do prospecting on your behalf by sending emails. (Again, why pay you to prospect for me, when clearly you don't know if you are reaching out to the correct people?)

2) Reply me with your Target Industry, Geography & Titles, I will send you information that you were looking for. (Why would I do that? Because you are special?)

This way you will have enough time to focus on pure sales talk with your clients.

If you're not the right person to speak with in this regard, I'd appreciate if you would be so kind as to forward this email to the right person.

Regards,
[Salesperson]

Lesson 9: Recess

//

You can discover more about a person in an hour of play than in a year of conversation.

— Plato

Aren't trade shows your most favorite thing to do? Say what? Trade shows aren't? Well why the heck not? You have all those hot prospects held captive in the exhibit hall! They have to come see you to get your signature on a card that proves they visited a certain number of booths and qualifies them for a raffle of a gift card or iPod. What could be better than competing with your competitors and other vendors for five minutes of a prospect's time?

Getting your fingernails pulled off with pliers, attending a second-grade recital or sitting through yet another sales meeting? Give you anything but "floor time." So why do most salespeople hate trade shows so much? It's not because they don't like visiting with prospects. It's because most sales and marketing managers go at trade shows all wrong.

Indeed, there are different types of trade shows. There are shows where actual meetings take place and deals get signed. Shows with meeting spaces within those booths were stuff gets done. If you attend those types of shows then you will enjoy this chapter because you can snicker about the poor suckers who have attended "the other kind." You will also learn lots about how to make the shows where you have private in-booth appointments even more productive.

The other trade shows are where you might as well be a shop owner in the tourist section of a Mexican town. You know, trade shows where there's row after row of 10-by-10 booths with food in the back of the hall to entice attendees to brave the sensory onslaught of hungry "me first" salespeople?

Tourists actually choose to subject themselves to the Mexican market district bombardment. Hey, you gotta get a drink! And like a trade show the restaurant Cabo Wabo is deep in the desperate salesperson doo-doo. But you don't have to go to Cabo to find such a land of sales sharks. Cancun, Acapulco, Rocky Point (which we Phoenicians think we own) or any other tourist stop has them. This is where the cruise ship dumps you or you might go when you dare venture out of your resort to see the "real Mexico."

First, you stop for a few Bloody Marys or Tequila Sunrises to help fend off remnants of the night before or get your vacation-inspired buzz banging again. Then it's time to dive into the shops for cheap crap to bring back to your kids, relatives, friends and lucky co-workers. Feeling the Cabo Wabo Tequila love, you venture into your first shop to find a lovely assortment of profane T-shirts, pottery, tiles, sombreros, mugs, cheap toys and Mexican blankets. That shot glass might be the perfect gift for your cubemate. But of course you aren't going to buy in the first place you visit, so you take your buzz on to the next store where you find more of the same cheap crap. Hummm.

Venture back on the street and you will see a ton of similar shops basically hawking the same crap. The first few shops are kind of amusing, especially when you factor in the friendly shopkeepers offering you a "great deal." But as you walk down the street, the previously amusing pleading turns into an overwhelming cacophony of economic desperation.

"Come in my shop!"

"Almost free!"

"I make you a good deal!"

"Best deals here!"

"You want gold? Pottery? Blanket? Come in!"

"Come in!"

"Hey, amigo! Cheap stuff! Almost free!"

"Good quality! Cheap!"

Shit! You need another drink! And with everyone offering the same crap at seemingly cheaper and cheaper prices, hell, almost free, why would you buy anyway if you might be able to find it cheaper at the next shop? And so you are left with confusion, cash in your pocket and general disdain for anyone calling you "amigo."

The Mexican tourist shopping experience sucks because the shopkeepers sell like bad second-graders. Is there any benefit to you at all in their pleadings to come on in? Nada, gringo. They just want your dineros even if the products are "almost free." Otherwise they wouldn't bug the heck out of you and instead offer something useful like free tequila. Seriously, what if they started a conversation by welcoming you to town or offering a free map of the area or even enticing you inside with a sign that says, "Our crap isn't almost free because it's good crap."

Even without the sign you could get a better experience with a shop that simply didn't play loud music and owners who didn't follow you around the store. Without the sensory bombardment you might have the time to think and decide to buy. It would certainly be a nice respite from the onslaught on the street.

Now, transport yourself from Cancun to the basement exhibit hall at the Marriott, Hilton, Sheraton or other mega hotel. Observe the lines of vendors in their 10 by 10s and watch when the attendees come in for coffee and cookies like a tourist seeking a Bloody Mary. Not too much different than a Mexican marketplace is it?

Think about it. There are lines of "shops" filled with salespeople who have sales quotas, maybe even quotas on how many people they need to talk to at the show. And those salespeople are desperate to talk to attendees. The salespeople will even give you "almost free" stuff to get you in the booth — stress balls, pens, Dove bars, mugs, iPod shuffles, Slinkys, chocolate, hats, umbrellas — you know, anything that can have a company logo printed on it. Why are those free souvenirs for your kids "almost free"? Because once you get your free trinket, the sale is on. Not for your benefit, but for theirs.

If you haven't gone to a trade show as an attendee, then you need to. If you can't do that, then step outside of your booth and observe. Or you can go to Mexico and shop, which is a little more fun because at least you have a buzz. Then again, maybe you are buzzed to cope at the trade show, too. Bad salesperson! Bad!

By completing one of the above, you will see what I'm talking about and will beg your boss to do something different to give trade show attendees a better experience. We're such copycats at trade shows, it's amazing. Send a postcard begging for folks to come by the booth (which rarely works), wait for them to walk by the booth, manage to make eye contact, offer some free stuff and then sell your brains out. And you wonder why attendees avoid you like Montezuma's revenge?

Some companies do it right at trade shows, provided the venue and the budgets are large enough. We're talking whopper trade shows like the National Association of Broadcasters where TV programming is bought and sold. At those shows a 40-by-40-foot booth is of moderate size. Large companies make two-story booths that are thousands of square feet and have amazing perks like small restaurants run by celebrity chefs. They also have quiet meeting areas away from all the throngs. It's not much different from a private airport lounge or the VIP area of a busy restaurant or bar. Don't you feel special and more relaxed when you hang out in one of those places? And when you are pampered, treated special or have a unique experience, you are more likely to buy.

There may be some of you who are thinking, "Yeah, that's all good and well but I don't have a massive trade show budget especially in this economy. Like I could do that?" So true! The good news is you don't need a ginormous budget to give your prospects a truly special trade show experience. You can do it on a shoestring, or a budget much smaller than the one you had last year, but only if you understand the psychology behind what people need at trade shows.

The body and the psyche can only take so much until you are contributing to the sensory overstimulation. You should be treating trade show attendees like they are second-graders because classroom environments are engineered to generate the best results. And that means eliminating overstimulation. And guess what? It ain't much different when you grow up.

Go to any second-grade classroom and you will immediately notice there is no loud noise, flashing lights, piles of candy or other things that could distract the students. If it's a well-maintained and designed classroom, even the clutter on the walls is kept to a minimum. And it's no wonder. Ask any education expert and the person will tell you that loud noises and clutter detract from the learning environment.

"Safe and Healthy School Environments" — a recent article in Pediatric Clinics of North America written by a handful of doctors — might as well be your bible for trade show setups. As you will soon see, you are not that far removed from rug rats. Let's start with lighting, which is notoriously abysmal at trade shows.

"A comprehensive approach to optimal lighting includes using daylight and providing outdoor views in all classrooms and work areas, combining daylight and electric lighting to prevent shadows and areas of poor illumination during cloudy days or during darkness, and the addition of flexible lighting controls. A direct correlation between student learning and lighting quality has been demonstrated in a study of three school districts. Students with more daylight in their classrooms progressed more than 20 percent faster in math and reading skills than their counterparts in classrooms without daylight."[26]

Why did the students do so much better? The authors couldn't point it out for sure. That said, all the theories boil down to ... you guessed it ... because students had natural light. If you poor suckers who live in an area up north get bummed out after a winter of low light and "concrete sky", it only makes sense that bright natural light would improve your mood. Aside from the cerveza, don't you feel better the instant you hit the beach on a winter vacation? Kids react the same way in the classroom. No matter what your age, natural light helps.

Many places that were akin to crypts are now being reborn with natural light. Newly constructed hospitals have "healing environments" with atriums and floor-to-ceiling windows. New airport terminals are becoming giant atriums; heck, even the new north terminal at the Detroit Metropolitan Wayne County Airport is bathed in natural light, an enormous departure from the L.C. Smith and Barry terminals it replaced, both of which resembled run-down Manhattan subway stations. The new terminal even has a gigantic marble fountain in the middle. It's so nice you actually don't mind hanging out there ... in Detroit. If Detroit can get it right, God knows anyone can.

Remember the Vegas casinos — those large caverns of gaming madness with no windows? Conventional wisdom says if the outside world is eliminated, gamblers will lose track of time and lose lots more money. It's been the norm in casino design for like, ever. Leave it to Vegas trailblazer Steve Wynn to shatter that notion. His multibillion-dollar resort Encore is based around natural light, even in the casino. Some reports mention "Wynndows" — glass developed to allow the outside in, but not reflect the interior lights. That's a huge bet that Mother Nature will deliver a jackpot, and Wynn and his talented team have rarely if ever placed a bad bet. Fact is they have consistently brought down the house.

Yet trade shows are normally in the dungeon of the hotel — you know, that bottom, bottom floor where you can see the sewer pipes and AC ducts running along the ceiling? Yep, that one! Or in big convention halls with windows about a mile away. The Sands Expo and Convention Center in Vegas or the New Orleans Morial Convention Center come to mind. Tombs so big you need a bike or golf cart to get around.

Wynn Resorts plans on building a giant convention center of its own behind Wynn and Encore. It will be interesting to see if those too are designed with "Wynndows." Since many hotel designers follow Wynn's lead, perhaps new convention centers will follow if the Wynn team goes for natural light in the new convention center.

In such an inhospitable environment, it's no wonder why all you want to do is curl up in the fetal position on a hotel comforter after a day on the convention floor. Well, if it isn't the poor lighting that is sapping your spirits and sabotaging your sales strategy, if just might be the noise.

"The most consistent finding is that the effects of chronic noise on learning are most pronounced when a task or activity is difficult or complex or when greater concentration is needed. ... Health issues related to classroom noise include stress and increased blood pressure and heart rates in children — conditions that may persist into adulthood."

Oh yes, the noise. Have you ever been in a quiet convention hall? Perhaps when it's empty. Even during setup and breakdown you're bombarded with vacuums, forklifts and other racket. Raising your voice at a prospect is not the freeway to sales love, yet that is what we do in convention halls. And chances are prospects can't hear everything you say but are just nodding with you as if they can. We all do that.

When it comes to classrooms, the good doctors are talking merely about noise from mechanical systems like air conditioning, the hallway or nearby music rooms. This is a far cry from the loudspeakers, people making loud conversation with friends, and salespeople trying to bark over all of it that you will find in a typical convention hall. As far as noise is concerned, if you are selling on a convention floor, you might as well be on the floor of a Vegas casino.

Casinos want you to be bombarded with all the lights and sound so you don't pay attention to the time and how much money you are losing. But if you only have a few minutes of time to spend with a prospect on the convention floor, don't you want the person to pay attention to your solution? With all that noise, it just ain't gonna happen.

One thing casinos do have dialed in is the temperature. Even if you don't gamble, if you have a chance, visit a casino and take note.

Chances are the temperature is Goldilocks — it's not too hot, not too cold, but just right. That's because temperature has much to with attentiveness and your mood. Everyone knows people get cranky and tired when it's too warm and stuffy in a room. Being cold can reduce people to babbling obsessions for warmth. It's no wonder that classroom experts recommend an ideal temperature of 69.8 to 73.4 degrees Fahrenheit with a relative humidity of 40 to 60 percent and good air movement.[27]

From my experience, convention halls, especially those in the basement, are either too hot or too cold and the air circulation is next to nothing. Well then, the quality of food in the hall certainly should contribute to an excellent sales environment, shouldn't it? Chocolate chip cookies, chips, sodas and other sugary and fat-laden treats are always available ... just like they were in schools. That is until the federal government stepped in.

Aside from the fact that readily available junk food was contributing to the tally of junior fat asses, there's a ton of evidence that shows it also makes kids uncooperative little freaks who have a tough time learning. Poor nutrition contributes not only to poor physical health but also to poor mental and cognitive health — the exact building blocks you need to pay attention and learn.[28] It doesn't take a bunch of scientists to figure this out but they did anyway to prove it once and for all. And besides the federal government was paying for it so why not?

The study, "Learning Connection: The Value of Improving Nutrition and Physical Activity in Our Schools," published by Action for Healthy Kids, outlines these findings and some success stories about how changing the downward spiral of nutritional nothingness can really help kids. One of those success stories illustrates just how whacked out kids get when they sustain themselves on sugar and high-fat foods. A school in Montana noticed that most behavioral problems occurred 40 to 60 minutes after lunch. That lunch, it was noted, contained high sugar and fats.

So the school eliminated sodas and other sugary junk and improved the menu. Instead kids were fed salads, fruits, sandwiches, yogurt and other healthy stuff washed down with water, low-fat milk or 100 percent fruit juice. Within two years, "disciplinary referrals" went from as many as eight per day to just one or two per week.[29]

Yes, but you are an adult who can handle a few sugar spikes here and there, right? Nope. Even little variations in blood sugar can cause problems for cognition. Previously you learned how low glucose can really make a mess of presentations and your overall performance — that's been known for awhile. Very recent research points to the effects high blood sugar can have on adult memory.

Ever wonder why the older you get, the more you forget stuff? It could have much to do with even moderate increases in blood sugar. Researchers at Columbia University Medical Center discovered that it's tougher for us to concentrate when sugar goes up. And the older we get the more difficult it is for our bodies to regulate blood glucose. This has huge implications for people with type 2 diabetes, but even for us "normal" folks it can be important.

Scientists using MRI diagnostics correlated increased glucose levels with decreased blood flow in the brains of elderly adults. Elevated sugar levels don't just adversely affect the brain function of elderly and those with type 2 diabetes, though. According to this study, it affects everyone and the older you get the worse it becomes. What's the recommended treatment? Exercise. You will learn more about that in the P.E. section. You think eating less raw sugar might work too? Yeah, so do I.

If you are now thinking that all that junk affects how children and adults learn and process information, give yourself a big old Blondie Sundae on me! Oh man, those are good, especially when the Blondie is nice and warm and they drizzle a little caramel on top. Score! Where was I? Oh yeah, the correlation between nutrition and learning.

Noise, heat, bad lighting and crappy food pile up quickly to wear you down and wear you out. As if trade shows aren't bad enough, guess what? It gets even worse! Yes, indeed, boys and girls, because when prospects come tripping into the land of business bombardment they are already experiencing cognitive fatigue.

Cognitive fatigue is generally defined as: "the unwillingness of alert, motivated subjects to continue performance of mental work."[30] You know, like when a prospect just sat through a seminar or has roamed the floor for hours and you expect them to be engaged in your bloviating about your product when all they really want is the free squeezy ball to take to their kids?

Scientists at the NASA Ames Research Center did research on cognitive fatigue by slapping EEG sensors on the noggins of 33 volunteers and making them do simple math problems until their brains exploded. Seriously, they did slap EEG sensors on volunteers and had them do math problems, to get an idea of just how long people could concentrate on a task before their brain started to literally shut down.

This is important to NASA because astronauts have to do tasks in space for hours on end with little room for error. It should be important to you because everyone's brain is pretty much the same. Even similar to someone who has the honor of sharing a space station with a Russian. As well, once you are cognitively pooped, you won't perform very well and neither will your prospect so you should know what that kind of tired is and how to avoid it.

Back to the experiment. Of those 33 volunteers, only 16 had useable data. Some washed out because there was interference within the EEG, others because they wore a watch and some others because they fell asleep — my personal favorite. While videotaped, these subjects sat in front of a computer and did four-digit math problems like "$4 + 7 - 5 + 2 = 8$" on a keypad. They were asked to solve the problems by indicating if each was greater than, less than or equal to the sum. After a one-second break, another problem was presented. This process was repeated until the subject gave up or three hours passed. Hell for most but hey, the volunteers got paid.

Scientists measured the effects of this test in three different ways: by questioning the volunteers, observing them and reading the EEGs. All three indicated that test subjects were mentally whipped by this simple task.

Test subjects reported that their energy level went down along with "calmness." What went up? "General deactivation" or the feeling of being tired. One thing that didn't change was mood. So even though the test subjects were tired and not that calm, they weren't cranky.

Observations revealed that the cognitive fatigue was much more severe than the subjects self-reported. Alertness decreased by more than half from start to finish. As the hours passed it also took longer for subjects to do each problem. In the beginning answers were given around six seconds per problem. By the end it took roughly 7.5 seconds. That said, the accuracy of the answers was not significantly affected by time.

The EEG results indicated that as time went on subjects literally became more dreamy and relaxed. Alpha waves were measured in the brain and as the tests went on those waves increased significantly. According to answers.com, alpha waves are "related to relaxation and a dreamlike state." One can only assume that as the tests went on, the subjects' brains started directing them to nappy time and both the self-reported and the observations support this.

Maybe that's why classroom lessons are usually less than an hour and you start losing focus in a meeting of the same length. Or attendees are spent just a few hours into a day at the trade show.

Poor lighting, noise, uncomfortable temperatures and low nutritional value food — it's convention time! Have you ever been to an important internal meeting in a hot sticky room with dim florescent lights and noise while washing down a cookie with a soda? OK, maybe the last part but not everything else. The reason is because supposedly you are there to think and get things done.

So why do we spend tens of thousands to exhibit at trade shows that resemble a birthday party at Chuck E. Cheese's? Because everyone else does? That seems to be the reason when I ask around. People seem to be afraid of being the company that doesn't show.

There might be some merit to that. And admittedly there usually are some leads to be gained and business to be done even in horrible trade show conditions. But that doesn't mean they can't be better and you can't gain a competitive advantage by doing things differently than your competitors. Why should you be a follower?

Go to the show, but then do something completely different.

How different? That depends on your budget, creativity and how much your boss will trust you to try something new. To start, have you ever gone to scope out a trade show location months, perhaps a year before the show? That is step one to get your ideas together. If you don't do that, then your creative ideas will be crushed.

Second, have you ever asked your current customers or prospects what they want from you at the show? If not, why? You would be surprised at the answers. Once you do those two things, then you can change the game in your favor. Stack the odds, like controlling the variables of a sale so you create an "us" and "them" environment between you and your competitors.

On the trade show floor you can get swallowed up in the Mexican market world of sameness. What you have to do is get to people when they are off the floor. You can do that in a quiet way like setting up an Internet lounge or quiet area removed from the madness, maybe in an outside courtyard area where your message is subtle but relays "we care for you and we care more than those desperate assholes trying to sell you something in the convention hall." You can deliver something meaningful and useful to them — not just some random piece of cheap plastic promotional item with the company name plastered all over it. Or you can capitalize on one thing both second-graders and adults love — recess.

After being cooped up all day long in the classroom in a convention hall or — gasp! — sitting through lectures, people young and old need to let their hair down. I would argue that one of the main reasons folks like trade shows is that it gives them a chance to get away from the nagging at home and let loose in a strange city just like the old days! If you and your company own that, you are golden.

In the early '90s when I was first cutting my teeth in trade show land, I managed to crash the biggest party at the big Radio and Television News Directors Association (RTNDA) show — the coveted and needed-to-know-someone-to-get-in party thrown by CNN. Yes, that CNN. They make lots of money selling their news feeds to local TV stations across the country. CNN was so beyond the trade show floor, they weren't even on it. Instead, the company had its very own air-conditioned tent with nice carpeting, quiet areas, natural light and a temperature that was Goldilocks.

Yes, CNN is CNN and you don't have the mondo budget it does, but you can have the same impact on a shoestring. Promise. Oh, back to the "recess" part. So somehow I got into the big CNN bash, where you had to be invited and show your credential with photo ID. The party was spectacular and everyone who CNN wanted to be there, was there except, well … me. There was no selling and hardly any promotion but everyone knew who was picking up the tab and creating the coolest adult playground, at least at that show. And, oh, yes, it was all free. And all the other vendors who stuck to the rules were rammed in their 10 by 10s handing out promotional items. With CNN on a whole different level.

A friend of mine eventually moved up at the news giant, so for years I was an "official" guest at the events and every year, CNN owned the show just because of recess. People went to the show just for that party, which I'm sure delighted the RTNDA show organizers to no end. Every year CNN would show up, throw an epic bash with the likes of Huey Lewis and the News, REO Speedwagon and other '80s acts. I don't know what the return on investment was for

CNN, but considering the company did it year after year, I imagine it was substantial.

So if you are thinking, "Well, duh! Anyone can throw a party," then you are missing the point: There are parties and then there are parties that make money. Parties or events that convey the culture and professionalism of the company putting it on. An event like that could arguably make a head honcho a hero or a zero. The details are that vital. CNN had the deep pockets to hire event companies who could haul in thousands of dollars worth of lighting, yards of fabric, come up with the concept, book the act and make it all happen. But what about your company?

In 2006, my bosses at McMurry had the guts to let me spearhead something that was risky but could pay huge dividends — host a big party and concert on our campus with a live act. Yes, we were taking a page from the CNN playbook, but to have the guests — prospects who were in Phoenix for the big convention — there on our campus, away from most of the other sucker competitors who were worried about their booths and about making sure the preconvention postcard was mailed out on time — that was worth the risk.

Since we didn't have the budget for crazy party planners we created several committees and tackled it ourselves. Everything from the catering, bars and decorating, to negotiating with the talent and coordinating the sound and staging, to transportation to and from the convention to our campus. By event time, we had turned the campus into a sparkling concert venue, beautifully catered with seating for hundreds. It was a huge team accomplishment that took tons of planning, lots of Tums, Starbucks and an occasional Grey Goose on the rocks with lime. That said, early in that planning we decided on one thing that wouldn't happen at the event: selling.

I was the VP of sales for goodness' sake! How could it be that we shouldn't sell! It sure was a gut check. With all those people there waiting for '80s rock star Rick Springfield it wouldn't hurt to play an eensy-weensy little video about all the stuff we wanted them to buy, would it? How bad would it had sucked if your teacher strolled out and started a lesson in the middle of a recess game of burn ball (or butts up or whatever you called it)? It would have majorly sucked ass! You would have felt shortchanged. Even an invite to the booth would have felt yucky.

Nope, there would be no selling, not even a peep. Instead we invited people to take a tour of the campus for a chance to win a signed guitar from Rick. People were skeptical about that. You know how time shares offer you a free stay as long as you sit through the hard sell? That's what the guests were waiting for. The catch, the arm twisting, the "if you buy tonight."

Imagine their surprise when the twist never happened. Imagine how cool it was when instead they learned about the company values, how McMurry supported neighbors around us with free flu shots, helped repair their homes, sponsored neighborhood watches and transformed a run-down garbage alley into a beautiful, well-lit meandering park? Our guests weren't expecting heartfelt stories about our own charity to combat domestic violence and they certainly didn't expect our owner to be handing out hundred-dollar bills if a guest could recite the mission statement.

But the real secret weapon of the night was the employees. Does your company say the most valuable asset is its employees? Have you ever given everyone from the front desk and mailroom person to the CEO the opportunity to interact unscripted with customers, demonstrate the service you provide and party with complete strangers who had never sampled your company before? We did because we trust everyone who is on the team to do the right thing. And man, did they, each with an identifying shirt simply reading: STAFF.

So at an event like this, you'd be sure to exclude competitors, right? Heck, no! Any competitor could come, but unlike prospects and clients, competitors had to fork over $100 per person for the pleasure of showing up on our campus and getting schooled on how to treat customers. How many times has a competitor paid you? That was sweet!

If a competitor brought one of their clients, so much the better. How could a competitor compete? In fact, some of those competitor clients started working with us shortly thereafter. To them, it was like leaving a small town, going to the big city and saying, "Damn, look what I've been missing." The logistics were great, the food amazing, drinks a-plenty and Rick put on an amazing show which included heading out into the audience to the delight of the liquored-up ladies in the audience.

Recess cost us about $200,000. We generated more than $2 million in new sales as a result. We're talking sales to people who had never thought of using us before. Years later people who attended were still raving and those who didn't go wished they had. It's hard to calculate how much money we made indirectly from the event. Beyond that McMurry was officially "in the head" of our competitors. We know because they told us.

From then on at the big conventions, we spent the majority of our budget not on the stupid booth and squeezy toys we were going to give away, but on recess. Because as Plato said, "You can discover more about a person in an hour of play than in a year of conversation." Man, he was a smart dude.

Homework:

After your next convention, ask your boss to name five companies he didn't previously know about and what they sold. Can't name five? Okay, three then. Once he stumbles on that, give him a copy of this chapter along with ideas to get off the convention floor.

Crappy Cold Call: Lost in Translation

Dear Chad,

Hope this e-mail finds the best of your health and spirits. **(Like you care, Dude.)**

I would like to introduce myself as [Name] from [Company]. We would take it as an honor to be a part of your IT Vendor Management programme. **(Selling domestically is tough enough. Try selling internationally! You gotta feel for this guy.)** *I am sure, with amount of experience and exposure we have, we would be in a position to suffice most of your IT needs with the best of our resources. I would really appreciate if there could be any possibility to consider a basic level evaluation to engage [Company] as one of your preferred IT vendors.*

We provide business equipment, technical support and integrated software applications that save time and money and increase employee productivity. I would really appreciate if there could be any possibility to consider a basic level evaluation to engage [Company] as one of your preferred IT vendors.

Our Expertise: (And now...time to cut and paste the list!)

- *Collaboration: Microsoft SharePoint, ZSL Soc Net Solution, AJAX, Silverlight, Portals, Flash, Flex, Mash-up*
- *CRM: Microsoft CRM, Sale force, Sugar CRM, Microsoft Dynamics Suite, MS Dynamics GP, NAV, SL, & SBF, Infor, SAP*
- *Mobile Technologies: CRM Solutions on Windows Mobile, I-Phone, Blackberry, Google Android G1 Phones*
- *Migration: Client/Server to Web, Legacy to Web, Database to Web, PowerBuilder Migration*
- *Platforms: Microsoft .Net, Java Enterprise, PHP, Database Technologies*
- *Reporting tools: Business Intelligence, Data warehousing, Data Mining.*
- *Staffing Services: Contract basis- Onsite/offsite/Near shore Monthly resource billing model (160hrs)*
- *Cloud Services & Virtualization: Amazon Cloud services, VM Ware, SaaS.*
- *Other Areas: SOA, 21 CFR Part 11, HL7, EMR, EHR, PHR, Customization, CRM Add-ons, upgrades, re-licensing.*
- *Partnered with major technology providers Microsoft Gold certified Partner, IBM, Oracle, Red Hat, and Sun Microsystems. Please let me know if we can be of any help.*

We will only need 1/2 an hour of your time to present and answer any question you will have. Please let me know what dates and times would work best for your team. If those weeks do not work for you, (What weeks are we talking about again?)

please let me know what would better suit your schedule.

If a webinar would work best at this time, please let me know and I will make that happen as well.

We look forward to being of service to you!

PS: Avail up to 40% New Sign up discount for all qualified business with [Company] till 05th Feb 10. (If the list doesn't show me the value of working with this company tossing in a discount right from the start certainly will!)

Warmest Regards,
[Salesperson]

Lesson 10: Teacher Appreciation: Outliers on the Curve

//

Teacher, stop that screamin'. Teacher, don't you see?
Don't want to be no uptown fool.
— Van Halen

Think back to your days in school. You knew many kids — perhaps 30 per class, most of whom you couldn't remember if you tried. But there was another person in the classroom who you could most likely remember — your teachers. Teachers could burn good or bad into your brain like a branding iron.

If you were a typical student then most of your teachers fell into the "average" category. That's just the way it goes in life — most people are average. Chances are those average teachers faded from memory like most of your classmates. Who made the greatest impression? Probably the worst or the best of the lot — the outliers on the curve. You know the teacher who sucked, hated life, maybe had mental issues and took it out on the class. Or the inspirational ones who gave because giving was in their nature.

To this day I remember my idiot second-grade teacher who allowed another student to make me stare at the glare of a white wall in the sun because of some kind of recess infraction. I ended up having to wear dark glasses because my retinas were burned. Then there was my high school music teacher, Mr. Compher, who encouraged me to sing as much as possible and helped me hone my skills — I made thousands of dollars and had incredible experiences as a result and still sing to this day.

Another high school teacher who knew my friends and I were drunk in class and did nothing about it — looking back now, I realize how horrible she was. Then there was my high school English teacher, Mrs. Hadley, who inspired me to write. Other than that handful, both good and bad, the rest were faceless people who handed me grades. Unfortunate but true.

Students play a role in the classroom environment too. And we will chat about your responsibility as a student of sales soon. But for now, let's focus on the teacher. We'll get to the student behavior protocol later. Promise.

The Council of Chief State School Officers grants the "Teacher of the Year" to one outstanding teacher. The year 2008 marked the 58th consecutive award. To be considered for this honor, a teacher must first have won the state or "extra-state" teacher of the year award, which is an impressive achievement on its own. Those 55 top teachers submit written applications full of essays and letters of recommendations. A selection committee, consisting of members of top education and child development associations and federations, selects the winner. Then the president of the United States awards the prize. Huge deal.

In 2008, the winner was Michael Geisen, a seventh-grade science teacher from Prineville, Ore. Haven't heard of Prineville? Join the club! For you geographic types, the "city" is roughly southeast of Portland and a little northeast of Bend. Data from 2007 puts the population at 8,720 people. The most common occupation is in wood products followed by construction, motor vehicle parts, agriculture, forestry, fishing and hunting. Just more than 15 percent of the population went beyond a high school education.[31] With those facts in mind, it's no wonder many of the students at Crook County Middle School come from low socioeconomic homes.

Lucky for those kids they have Mr. Geisen. Read his application and you won't find a teacher. What you will find is a genuinely humble, truly inspiring, servant leader. In that application, you will find numerous comments by Geisen that he is not the best at his craft, that there are better teachers and that he can always improve.

Central to his message isn't the fact that he wants to teach, but that he has a burning desire to give. And that a teacher's "greatest accomplishments [are] in the lives of [the] students."[32]

Forget about his impressive classroom and look at Geisen's accomplishments outside of it. Serving dinner to students and their families at special school events. Transforming a run-down courtyard on the school grounds into an outdoor "learning laboratory." Not only building a 1,000-foot climbing wall but securing the money, donations and doing all the planning to build it on his own time. Then teaching courses on how to rock climb. All on top of his normal teaching duties. Why such monumental efforts? According to Geisen, the efforts are to teach all of his "students."

"I quickly realized that middle school teachers are actually teachers of students, and that the subject matter was somewhat secondary. I am now starting to realize that our true job is actually teacher of the community."

This commitment to serving has inspired students to help solve worldwide problems as a direct result of Geisen's lessons. And in true form, Geisen helped the students raise money to assist with their endeavors.

Now if you are wondering why I'm gushing about Geisen and how that ties into sales, take a chill pill and keep reading. Why are we salespeople so damn antsy all the time? If you are squirming then go grab a Coke or stretch on the airplane and come back to the book because this is important. All this back story and Geisen's inspiration has everything to do with quite possibly the most important factor in your success other than your own personal effort — your boss. If you are lucky, you can call him or her your leader. If you are one in 100, you can look at your leader not as a boss but as a servant.

Geisen practices incredible servant leadership, apparently quite naturally. But servant leadership is tough to embrace and especially hard to master for pressured pinhead hierarchal managers. Especially sales managers. What's sad about that fact is that cultures have been preaching the benefits of servant leadership since, if not the beginning of time, then darn close and across many cultures.

The earliest incarnation came from the writings of the mysterious Laotzu. His teachings are the basis of Philosophical Taoism. Legend has it that even Confucius himself sought out Laotzu to learn some of his wisdom. And since Laotzu reportedly lived to the spry old age of nearly 1,000, he must have had loads of it. His swan song was a very short book — heck, you could call it a pamphlet — entitled the Tao Te Ching.

Like many massively influential books there is endless debate about both the origin of Tao Te Ching and if Laotzu even wrote it. Not too far-fetched considering the rather wacky (by modern standards) oral history of Laotzu himself. Like another religious figure you might have heard about, Laotzu was the product of immaculate conception — but in Lao's case from a shooting star. From there he gestated for 62 years until he popped out an old man.

He wandered around ancient China speaking his wisdom, but never wrote it down. Late in Laotzu's life he was fed up with man's inability to "use life with natural goodness" so he hopped on a water buffalo and high-tailed it to the desert. Eventually he came upon a man named Yin Hsi, fulfilling Hsi's dream. Hsi somehow convinced Laotzu to write down his philosophy. The result was

Tao Te Ching. "Tao meaning the way of all life, the fit use of life by men and ching a text or classic."

Or to put it in our vernacular: A classic book on how man should live. A bible, if you will. Actually Tao Te Ching is second only to the Bible in number of translations and has many philosophical similarities. After Laotzu completed his work, he got back on the buffalo and rode off into the distance never to be seen again.

Like the Bible, there's much controversy as to who actually wrote Tao Te Ching. There's no written history so it's impossible to determine a definitive answer. Some scholars consider Laotzu nothing more than a myth. Others contend that Tao Te Ching is actually a compilation of the writings of three Taoist sages written hundreds of years after Laotzu hauled ass on the buffalo. Then again, the sages could have been editors. No one knows for sure.[34]

What matters is the content of Tao Te Ching. Religious controversy aside, the philosophy simply makes sense. Read it and you will want to hug your neighbor, sit on a mountainside and just be. You will also realize how much you stress out on stuff that doesn't mean squat and the intrinsic goodness of giving.

Now I don't go around breaking into spontaneous "Kumbaya" singalongs, but the book does make sense in many facets of life, including leadership. The work has thrived for thousands of years, so there must be something to it, don't you think? The entire Tao Te Ching is everywhere on the Internet. Google it and read it for yourself. It's fascinating.

Here's how the Tao of servitude shakes out in three easy phrases.

"When the Master governs, the people are hardly aware that he exists. Next best is a leader who is loved. Next, one who is feared.

The worst is one who is despised."

"If you want to govern the people, you must place yourself below them. If you want to lead the people, you must learn how to follow them. If you don't trust the people, you make them untrustworthy."

"All streams flow to the sea because it is lower than they are. Humility gives it its power."

Another guy you may have heard of, talked about being a servant leader too. Over the years his philosophies have attracted about 2 billion followers. Even non-Christians recognize Jesus as a pretty smart guy. And here's what he said about being a servant to others:

"Whoever wants to be first must place himself last of all and be the servant of all." (Mark 9:35)

I doubt Laotzu or Jesus had salespeople in mind when discussing servitude, but like many great ideas theirs were so simply powerful that the ideas have stood the test of time and apply to many situations — yes, even sales and sales leadership.

Robert Greenleaf, a retired IBM executive, came up with his own servant philosophy that consciously or not carries the heart of Laotsu and Jesus' message. His groundbreaking essay, "The Power of Servant Leadership," lays out an argument for serving first. Greenleaf. org, an organization dedicated to servant leadership, sums up Greanleaf's philosophy like this:

"The servant-leader is servant first. ... It begins with the natural feeling that one wants to serve, to serve first. Then conscious choice brings one to aspire to lead. That person is sharply different from one who is leader first, perhaps because of the need to assuage an unusual power drive or to acquire material possessions. ... The leader-first and the servant-first are two extreme types. Between them there are shadings and blends that are part of the infinite variety of human nature."[35]

I doubt the bell curve from "leader-first to servant-first" is a classic line. Instead I would argue that it's heavily skewed left. There are far more "leaders" who are there for personal gain and glory first or to move things from point A to point B than there are true servant leaders. Let's call the individuals on the left "managers" who literally manage the expectations, numbers and short-term goals of salespeople. As you move toward the right, sales leaders become more accustomed to developing and leading than dictating regulation and checking off call reports, until you finally end up with a true servant leader like Geisen.

Does this mean servant leaders are not concerned with the end result? Of course not. What it does mean is that they see the bigger picture and instill the trust and faith in those they serve to get it done. For a teacher like Geisen or the teacher of a sales team, deciding to servant lead can take some serious soul searching. "Letting go" can be a huge leap of faith.

For Geisen, part of letting go is not using textbooks. Well, he does use them in a way — for classroom decoration. Instead, he tailors his lessons to the students, the times and what will appeal to them. He treats them like equals even though they are in seventh grade. And he tries to change the way he teaches and to continually get better. "A great teacher is a unifier, as well. A unifier of ideas, a unifier of people and a unifier of ideas with people."

"I make it a goal to greet students each day as they enter, call them by name as often as possible, and to use humor to break down barriers of class, race, age and ability. I want to have a unique and meaningful relationship with each of my students. This is really the heart of teaching."[36]

No scripts, humor, serving, unique and meaningful relationships. Huh, this guy might be on to something!

Teachers like Geisen are a rare find. Ask any CEO or human resources VP and they will tell you one of the hardest positions to fill in business is that of a sales leader. The reason speaks to the message throughout this book: We salespeople are very selfish and we need to get over it. Why wouldn't we be selfish? We are here to sell and make as much money for ourselves as possible. But as you have read, that "me first" strategy will only get you in the average zone at best. To break on through to the right you have to become a sales servant.

Achieving that is a bitch. It forces us to change our very nature, which takes tons of effort and self-reflection. If you have an arrogant, power-hungry leader, your path to wealth will be even more treacherous. How do I know? I worked for one of those pricks. More on that later.

Sales leaders are tough to find because there are so few servant salespeople. And you CANNOT be an effective sales leader if you don't first know how to serve. Companies continually make the mistake of assuming that the dynamite salesperson will be a dynamite sales leader, but rarely are the skill sets the same.

Incredible salespeople may very well have taught themselves to come off as servants to their customers. And maybe they actually are as long as the big score is in sight. These lone wolves do fine, but hem them in with a pack and fur can quickly fly. Why is that? Hate to get all geeky on you because I'm not (OK, maybe a little bit), but it all boils down to "The Force."

Yes as in "Star Wars" the Force. Remember the old first "Star Wars," which was actually part four of the six-part series because they had to start in the middle due to the special effects restrictions of the day? At least that's what I heard.

Anyway, toward the end of the movie, if you recall, Luke is trying to land a fatal shot to the Death Star. He tries to use the computer guidance system to no avail. Then you hear Obi-Wan Kenobi urging Luke to use "The Force" and "Let Go" — in other words, "have faith, oh, auditory hallucinator!" Luke shoots without the computer, nails the Death Star, figures he gets the girl (which is actually his sister, ewwwww!) and they all live happily until Darth Vader shows up again but really pissed off this time. Sales leadership is kind of like that.

What most selfish salespeople can't manage is the whole "letting go" part. We control our destinies and can't handle not trying to get our way. It's what causes salespeople to make self-centered crappy cold calls. And it's the driving force behind sales managers demanding call sheets, reports, explanations, copious notes in Salesforce and phone logs. They can't darn well let go and convey the trust salespeople should be conveying to their prospects.

Say what!? Without reports, logs and other nit-picky time-wasting drudgery how would a sales manager know the team is doing what it's supposed to? It's called sales, doofus. Gee, if a rep isn't making sales, do you think they are doing those other things?

So when sales superstars get promoted to management, they do what salespeople do — try to control everything. On top of that, the upper management demands some kind of data to assure them that ROI is coming from their investment in labor, so they better see "some numbers" and you know what rolls downhill.

Buck that trend, like Luke did when he shut down his targeting computer, and chances are a sales manager will get the same, "Crap, we're all doomed!" reaction the commanders at base showed. So come to think of it, sales leadership impotence has to do with control freak promoted salespeople and the nervous bosses above them who have nothing better to do than ask for "activity" reports.

To illustrate this nightmare, let me introduce you to Bob (name changed). In 1999, Bob was a newly minted sales manager at the company I worked for. He had been good at selling in his own right, mostly in the old-school method of pitting two potential buyers against each other, but, hey, he got things done. I was one of his first new hires.

Now no one has ever called me "meek" by any means — arrogant would be more like it — and back then I was not only arrogant but I was young and foolish to boot. Bob had his hands full from the start, not just teaching me how to sell what the company sold, but keeping my temper and ambitions in check.

In the beginning he did a good job and we had a couple of good, productive years together. But then things went rapidly downhill. While it's hard to put a finger on why, the relationship fell apart. It went from trusting to adversarial. Suddenly he wasn't with us, he was against us. And I mean all the salespeople.

Most days he was locked in his office and if you asked for help, it was half-assed and sullen. Honestly, I think he was going through some pretty serious personal problems that were beyond our imagination. People have bad years and problems at home. It happens. But when an employee starts taking it out on others that's when there's a problem. And that is exactly what happened.

Because he was essentially failing at his job by not leading adequately and not getting sales, Bob went into "preservation" mode. He started firing salespeople to show he was doing something and worse than that, handing out bad advice so salespeople would fail. Hey, it was better to maintain the position he had and lose a few bonuses than lose a job altogether. And that's when he started targeting me as next on the list.

We battled a lot. Publicly. It was embarrassing and not professional, but it happened. I'm surprised both of us didn't get fired in the process. Maybe his bosses knew more than I did — most likely so. It was tough to ignore what was going on around us because the environment in the sales office was nasty.

What pushed me to the edge was when he sold a deal out from under me. That ever happen to you? To add insult he unfairly kept for himself three-quarters of a commission I had earned on another deal. But that wasn't it for the sales manager from hell — or perhaps a sales manager that sounds eerily familiar to yours.

The epic meltdown happened at our biggest convention of the year. We were in Dallas with a bunch of clients — health care marketers to be exact — and taking them out for a night on the town. Our fearless leader who by then had pounded down several vodkas had arranged for dinner and dancing. One stretch limo showed up to whisk away 15 of us jammed in like motoring clowns at the circus. We laughed it off with the clients and besides the ride to the steakhouse was short.

Dinner was delicious. The clients were thrilled. A few were even smart enough to catch their own ride back to the hotel. The rest of us clowns got stuffed back into the limo with Bob — drunker on vodka than Boris Yeltsin. Just like a clown car we started driving in circles searching for someplace to "partayyyyyy!"

The limo was hot. Everyone was squished. And we were in some seedy section of Dallas with no sense of direction and a clown captain who couldn't see straight. That's when the Bob bitch slapped the partayyyyy.

Bob screamed, "Stop this @#$ing car!" to the driver. In a scene reminiscent of a bad reality show, Bob and the driver hopped out of the car and launched salvos of f-bomb-laced insults. The driver threatened to kick us out of the car, stranded. In Dallas.

Shit.

Somehow Bob talked him into driving to the next "joint," hopped back in the car and f-bommed the driver until we got to the skankiest blues bar that side of Memphis. The clients were speechless and more fled for the nearest cab they could find. A few other gluttons including me and the other hapless and speechless salesmen watched as Bob tried to salvage the night by forcing people to dance with him on the dingy dance floor.

Partayyyyy!

The next day when everyone was at the convention floor but him, we the salespeople in order to form a more perfect union decided we had to mutiny. You see the clown car limo ride with a stop at reality TV world complete with the f-bomb explosion and the seedy blues bar wasn't enough. We had to spend our time apologizing to the parade of clients mortified by their Dallas adventure.

Bob getting even drunker at the hotel bar and causing a scene that same night didn't help. He hit bottom. And for a guy who survived for the better part of a year by setting people up for failure and then firing people, he had it coming. So I took it upon myself to go to the principal (Bob's boss) and tattle like crazy. Warning: don't ever do this yourself unless you are prepared to nearly lose your job in the process. After all, your shit stinks, too and the brass will point it out. Just like a teacher when you tattled in second grade.

A couple of very stressful months went by and finally Bob resigned — I would imagine under some pressure from the bosses. Then the recipient of the "watch what you ask for" special was me. Now it was my turn to be boss and the first order of business was to keep the other guys who didn't get the promotion from quitting followed by turning sales around.

Partayyyy!!!

Bob had shown two sides of the leadership coin. At first he was a pretty good servant leader, but then he turned into the antithesis. Behavior to avoid had been on graphic display in Ketel One Vodka-fueled tirades and sacrificial firings. Servant leadership was absolutely the way to go and opposite of what Bob did except perhaps his first year. So does that mean that servant leaders let followers walk all over them? Not at all. How to effectively servant lead boils down to one basic concept. Keeping salespeople "on the crab." No homework today! We're going on a field trip!

Lesson 11: Field Trip

//

"Hey, Cameron. You realize if we played by the rules right now we'd be in gym?"

— Ferris Bueller

Wait just one second. This book is about Selling Like a Second-Grader, right? Absolutely and sometimes second-graders get to go on a field trip. So get your permission slips signed because we are going on a virtual field trip to the Bering Sea to watch brave men catch king and snow crabs. Oh yes, it has tons to do with leadership and sales.

You will see this virtual field trip on the Discovery Channel. Just tune in or set the DVR to record "Deadliest Catch." It's the best leadership show on television. Discovery.com has lots of cool stuff about the show online, including brief bios, games and video clips. Unfortunately, they don't air full episodes online yet so you will have to settle for the tube until they get a clue.

If you aren't familiar with the show, "Deadliest Catch" follows several crews of commercial fisherman during Alaskan king crab season and then snow (opilio) crab season. The "deadly" part comes from the fact that this type of commercial fishing is the deadliest job in the world — 26 times more deadly that the national average.[36] Even so, becoming a crab fisherman is very difficult unless you know someone. Despite the great danger and harsh conditions, the appeal is a potentially huge haul of money.

Crew members make between 1.5 and 10 percent of the profits. That could mean a paycheck as big as $50,000, even $100,000 for a week of backbreaking, mind-numbing work. While some fisherman hit huge bank like that, most don't and some even come home with nothing if the fishing is bad. Crew members can even come back losing money on expenses like food and personal gear. Average annual income is just under $30,000 for a fisherman. That's a far cry from 100 grand for one week. Kind of reminds you of sales, doesn't it?

Would it surprise you to find out that according to the U.S. Bureau of Labor Statistics the average pay of a sales representative was $59,121 to $74,073, depending on specialty?[37] Surely you are in sales to make much more than that! Maybe $300,000 or more perhaps? Bet that's one of the reasons why you got into sales in the first place — to make the big bucks, haul in the big catch. If you have been in it awhile, then you know some years are better than others. Just like crabbing.

The fishing grounds in the Bering Sea are home to storms so fierce they would be hurricanes in the Atlantic. Plying those seas are hundred-foot ships with a captain, engineer, deck boss and a handful of deckhands. The ships leave harbor with stacks of "crab pots" — giant rectangle crab traps that weigh about 800 pounds each.

After about an 18-hour cruise, the crew starts to drop pots in areas determined by the captain — many times in 10- to 20-foot seas of frigid water. It's a lot like dropping marketing messages and cold calls in the form of steel crab pots. Sometimes it will land on the crab and sometimes it won't. A crane operator picks up each pot and puts it on deck. Then a deckhand scrambles inside the pot with a bag of ground-up fish and a whole fish and hooks it into the pot. Hey, the crab have to snack on something!

Once this is complete the pot gets flipped overboard by a hydraulic lift. Another deckhand tosses a line attached to the pot overboard, along with some large buoys so the pot can be located later. Remember, this is all going on while the boat is pitching, heaving or rolling in the 42-degree seas.

Once the pots have "soaked" for a while — sometimes hours, sometimes days, the ships go back to pick up their bounty. This means throwing a grappling hook at the buoy, snagging the crab pot line, hooking it to a wench, hauling the pot to the side of the boat, then pulling the pot on top of the boat with the crane. Finally the crew opens the pot and sorts the crabs into keepers — that is if there are any. This process of setting pots and pulling pots, in the churning Bering Sea can go on for days straight. That's right, no breaks, no rest, little food. Relentless manual labor. And you thought your cold calls were tough.

Add all this up and there's no wonder people die doing this job. Let's count the ways:

- Getting crushed between crab pots or by falling equipment.
- Drowning by getting a foot caught in the line of a crab pot descending to the depths.
- Falling overboard and suffering from instant hypothermia.
- Sinking in heavy seas.
- Cracked skulls from falling ice.
- Screwing up because of sleep deprivation (see bullets 1–4)

Despite all these perils, everyone on the ship could come home from a fishing season without a dime of earnings. As previously mentioned, the crew could lose money on a trip because they have to pitch in for food. That's why when the boat gets "on the crab" the crew works beyond exhaustion to stuff the storage tanks full of the crawling bounty.

Is there a base salary for these stalwarts of the seas? Nope. Draw? Nope. That's right, straight commission, baby, 1.5 to 10 percent of the profits depending upon experience. No crab. No pay. Too bad. Shut up and fish.

Sales should be like that too.

Would it surprise you to hear that the captains are natural servant leaders? They literally hold the lives of the crew in their hands. Pilot the boat the wrong way and a wave could take out a crew member or worse, sink the ship. The captains also control the livelihood of the crew. If the captain doesn't get "on the crab," the crew could spend weeks futilely pulling up empty pots.

The captains of those ships keep their crew safe, give them the tools to catch crab and point the crew in the right direction. Their job is to captain the ship and give the crew the best opportunity to get the crab. You will never see the captains coddling crew members, especially new ones, and you will rarely if ever see them down on the deck helping a crew member do his job. Do the job as hard as you can or you are out.

The Hillstrand Brothers, co-captains of the "Time Bandit" commented at the start of the season while looking out on their crew, "One of those guys will be gone after this season. The person who does the worst is let go every year. I don't care if you are family or a friend. If you are at the bottom, 'bye-bye.'" No excuses; work your tail off even if you are new.

Each crew member gets a "share" of the profits from the season. New crew members or "greenhorns" get a portion of the share as voted on by the crew. If a greenhorn doesn't work hard he could end up with nothing. And the captain can take any portion of payment away if he sees fit.

Work hard. Get paid. No excuses.

So as servant leaders, the captain's job is to assure the crew's safety, keep order on the ship, find the crab and then push the crew to haul it all in. The captain also jumps in with solutions if something breaks — like the engine, crane or some other part of the boat. And the captain decides when a crew member isn't pulling his weight and works to change that behavior or else fire him. The captain is not there to hear excuses, whining or back down in the face of adversity. And this is absolutely not the captain's job: hauling in the crab. That's the job of the crew. The captain simply facilitates it.

On the boat dek, there's no shortage of stress, bickering and fighting like little kids. It could be viewed as a floating classroom at times with the students on deck and the teacher in the wheelhouse. From a leadership aspect it is also very similar to what a sales leader should be doing for you and what you should realistically expect from your sales leader. Just because your leader is a servant, doesn't mean he does your job for you.

A sales leader's job boils down to getting you on the crab. *That's it.* Then it is your responsibility to haul it in. The leader will also give you the tools to bring the crab and provide the means for you to get it. They should make sure you get there safely, settle any disputes with other crew members and offer a solution if something goes wrong. And one thing you will never see a Bering Sea captain ask for is a stupid call report.

Okay kids, let's hop back on the bus. It's time to get back to school for one last lesson.

Lesson 12: Report Card: S.I.C.K. S.H.I.T.

///

'Tis healthy to be sick sometimes.
— Henry David Thoreau

Now that you are nearing the end of your second stint in second grade, it's time for a stern warning about the cruel world: There's some S.I.C.K. S.H.I.T. going on in sales. Notice the acronyms? Good! Because they mean something! As you head out into the cold world of selling, these two acronyms will make or break you. If you copy anything down and post it on your desk, this should be it. But first a bit of back story.

As we have learned, salespeople practicing bad second-grade lessons succumb to self-fulfilling prophecies, cling to slicks, suffer the spotlight effect and the gonna happens — among other things. Nothing tells the story more than your report card. No, not your stupid end-of-the-year review (why your boss has to spend five pages and an hourlong meeting to tell you to "sell more" is beyond me). Nope, we're talking about your closing ratio at the end of the year. You know, the comparison between how many sales appointments you went on and how many of those you actually closed. That's your report card.

Like all report cards, this one shows your collective efforts for the entire year, and you can't go back in time. The grading scale would be a lot like baseball batting averages.

A: 30 – 35%

B: 20 – 29%

C: 10 – 19%

D: 2 – 9%

F: Quit sales for goodness' sake!

When it comes to closing ratio most salespeople would get a C for average — maybe 15 percent of appointments closed, tops. People who swear sales is "a numbers game" would be in the D range. The very crème de la crème of the sales crop would get an A. Let's make sure you get an A, too. That's where the S.I.C.K. S.H.I.T. comes in.

Ever seen the movie "Secondhand Lions"? You can rent it for $2.99 on iTunes, or buy it for $9.99. It's best to buy it, because trust me you will want to watch it again and again. The movie is also available on Netflix. Here's the official synopsis: "In 1960s Texas, timid teen Walter (Haley Joel Osment) is forced to spend the summer with his rich and eccentric great-uncles Garth and Hub (Michael Caine and Robert Duvall) on their farm, where, over time, Walter learns surprising tidbits about their mysterious and dangerous pasts."

It's a super fun movie even your real second-grader can watch (if you have one). What's surprising are the fantastic sales lessons! In 10 minutes you can learn how to bring your closing grade up and be entertained too. It's like *Math Circus* or *Schoolhouse Rock*. What could be better than that?

Without giving the movie away, Garth and Hub have amassed a fortune and don't spend a dime. They'd rather live a very simple life on their sprawling, run-down Texas farm. But the word is out: The old brothers are loaded, so surely they need to buy something. And that's when the salesmen come a cold calling. Old Garth and Hub make a sport of it as they sit on their front porch, sipping iced tea, shotguns in hand … waiting for a S.H.I.T. salesman to drive up.

Fast-forward to around 8:25 in the movie where you will find the first D student salesman. If you don't have the movie yet here's how the scene goes:

(Car approaches. Salesman gets out.)

Salesman: HEY! Rumor has it you have millions stashed away. Why not put some of that money to work for you with a high yield only investing in gold and silver can bring?

(Garth and Hub raise their shotguns and shoot.)

(Salesman runs behind car. Holds up pamphlet.)

Salesman: Can I leave you some pamphlets?

(Pamphlet gets shot out of his hand. Salesman floors it and drives off.)

(Garth and Hub reload their shotguns.)

(Second car approaches. Another salesman gets out.)

Salesman: Gentlemen, the word is out. You are two sophisticated men of means.

(Blam! Garth and Hub fire their guns.)

(Salesman screams. Drives off.)

(Reloading of guns.)

(Third salesman drives up. He opens his trunk to reveal a display of knives.)

(Garth and Hub fire shotguns.)

(Third salesman drives off.)

This brilliant under two-minute scene sums up the S.H.I.T that most salespeople do.

- Show up without a well-thought-out strategy
- Have nothing smart to say
- Imitate crappy salespeople
- Thank prospect and be forgotten

The first salesman steps out of the car, delivers a canned, scripted pitch, gets shot down and then breaks out his security blanket — the old pamphlet! Must be an "it's a numbers game" kind of guy. Grade: D

The second salesperson makes a half-assed observation and delivers nothing of value. He simply makes a general statement and gets shot down. Well, at least he doesn't go for a tired slick, so he gets a D+.

The third salesperson doesn't even try to say something. Nope, he goes straight for the product. Kind of like: "I want a new pair of shoes. Do you want to buy some toys?" Seriously? Grade: F — That "salesman" should hang it up.

Think about how you prospect and prepare for meetings. Then, think about how you cold call. Be honest, do the examples above seem familiar? If so, then you are never going to achieve the earnings you hope for in sales. There simply isn't enough time in the day, or prospects, to hit the numbers you want. You can't get an A by failing more and more tests. Grades just don't work that way.

I've heard bosses actually suggest that salespeople should pick up the phone and blindly dial away because "at some point they are going to get lucky and find someone who wants to buy." I wonder if they would tell their kids to "not study and just do your assignments and take tests. At some point you are going to get lucky." The answer is "NO!"

The reason is a matter of perception. Parents know there are only so many tests and assignments kids can do to get a good grade. Therefore, kids must study, prepare and make the best of every opportunity to get a good grade. Bosses mistakenly think there are unlimited opportunities to get a good grade in sales.

They are dead wrong.

Just like second-graders who get a string of bad grades, sales-people can only take so much negative feedback before self-doubt starts creeping in. Salespeople can only take getting shot down so many times before learned helplessness becomes the norm. "I just can't do it." "School is hard!" "Sales is too hard!" "I can't take any more rejection."

When the solution is quite simple. Just like assignments and tests, preparation gets you the A. Back to "Secondhand Lions," this time at about 23 minutes and 45 seconds into the film, for an illustration of this point. Here's how the scene basically goes, with lines taken directly from the movie:

(Horn honks. Salesman drives up, gets out, ducks behind fender and waves a white handkerchief.)

Salesman: Don't shoot! Don't shoot!

(Garth and Hub raise guns.)

Garth: He's been here before.

Salesman (still behind fender, waving handkerchief): Brothers McCann!

Garth: This is no ordinary salesman.

Hub: Yeah, I like me a challenge ...

Salesman: Can we talk?

Hub: Come out where we can see you!

Salesman: Put down your guns and I'll come out.

Garth (amused): This guy is good.

Hub: I'll cover, you sneak around.

Walter: Why don't you see what he's selling?

Hub: What the hell for?

Walter: What's the good of having all that money if you're never going to spend it?

Salesman: Trust me.

Hub to Garth: Could be the kid has a point. Let's see what the man is selling, then we'll shoot 'im.

Garth: Good plan.

(Walter, Hub and Garth step off porch and walk over to the salesman.)

Salesman: Whew! Due to the, uh, unsettling nature of our previous encounters I took it upon myself to search the world over for that perfect item that would be just right for two exuberant sportsmen such as yourselves. Well I do believe I've found it. (Pulls tarp off a large clay pigeon thrower). Wa la!

Walter: What is it?

Salesman: Well, that right there is the sport of kings. Up to now only heads of state have been able to afford a fine piece of equipment like that and it's so simple to operate even this child can do it.

Walter: Really?

Salesman: Tell you what, step right up here and chomp that lever back on my signal, OK? Go ahead.

(Walter pulls the lever and sends the clay pigeon flying. The salesman reaches in his trunk, pulls out a shotgun and shoots the pigeon out of the sky.)

Walter: Wow!

Salesman: The most powerful one on the market. Very reasonably priced I might add.

Hub: We'll take it.

(Hub and Garth start handing the salesman hundred-dollar bills.)

Wow! There's so much going on in that scene! There are countless lessons in it that will help you sell more. Let's start with how S.I.C.K. the last salesman was. Not sick as in ill, we're taking sick as in the definition from urbandictionary.com:

Sick: Crazy, cool, insane.

Or

• Study the prospect
• Invent a possible solution
• Check with them
• Kraft it for your meeting

As Garth said, this salesman was "good." He knew the brothers were a tough nut to crack and loved to fire shotguns. He knew they were going to shoot at him. He also knew that Walter was sitting on the porch too and could influence the deal.

Ah, the Walters in the sales world. Those "little" people who don't say much but could have great influence on a deal. Many salespeople overlook these "little" people — the executive assistant, the coordinator, the intern — but as that scene illustrates, those people can (and do) have tremendous influence on the buying decision.

Those low-level people can be the voice of reason, or the reason you don't get the deal. The salesman in the forth scene recognizes it. In fact, he anticipates and incorporates Walter into his pitch — "even a child can do it." When it comes to studying the prospect, Salesman #4 gets a solid "A."

Inventing a solution is the area where salespeople seem to trip up. That's all about the fear of rejection. Better to show up with a slick and charm to "build a relationship" than a well-thought-out idea. It's less risky that way. It's also the same effort other sales-people give. The reason: "Well, what if I'm wrong?"

Well, what if you are right? Or partially right. Or even completely off-base (which is doubtful if you studied the prospect)? The impression you will make on your prospect is that you took the time to offer something much more useful than your corporate B.S.

People are pressed for time. If they give you an hour of it, you better make it count. Showing up with a smart idea shows you value that time. It also makes your closing ratio grade go up because you are steps ahead of the sales cycle. Even if the solution you present is only partially correct, you at least have a baseline to talk about and a better place to start than your canned pitch and a supposed relationship. The fourth salesman in "Secondhand Lions" did this to a T, even going so far as to spend his own money to bring the solution. Nothing ventured, nothing gained.

He didn't check with the brothers before the pitch, however. This can be a critical part of inventing a solution, especially if you need to get on a plane or otherwise travel to present it. It's always good to know you are on the right track before you present your solution. Finding out if you are on the right track is as easy as firing off an email or picking up the phone. It goes something like this:

"Mr. or Ms. Prospect, to prepare for our meeting and make sure we make the most of your valuable time, why don't we talk about how (solution) can solve (need you have noticed). It would seem that if we solved that, you could (benefit). Would talking about that solution be valuable to you and a good use of your time?"

Sending an email or better yet getting the prospect on the phone for a few minutes does lots of things. It helps you start to turn off the spotlight effect and truly stand out from other salespeople. It shows that you are there to serve, not just to sell. It gives you an indication of just how interested the prospect is in you and your company/solution. It lets you know just how much time, effort and treasure you should spend to invent your solution.

When you check with the prospect, you may find that you are right on target, or a little off. You may get some coaching, which is a great thing. Or you may get the response that causes most salespeople to skip checking entirely: silence or outright rejection. Silence is a tough one. But outright rejection is great.

The silent treatment is the most confusing of all. It can mean the prospect really has no interest in you, is confusing you with another salesperson or worse, isn't there anymore! It can also mean the prospect is truly overwhelmed with work and you are just one item on an enormous list of things to do. It's at this point where you truly have to make an educated guess, kind of like what will be on a test in school.

Did you catch the prospect for like five seconds, set the meeting time and then never hear from the prospect again? You may want to reevaluate if you should spend your time meeting with the prospect in person. After all, you could use your effort on a better pitch. Did you spend a good amount of time talking to the prospect when you made your initial call or better yet did the prospect call in with serious interest? Then perhaps the silence just means something else is going on in and the prospect just can't get to you right now, but still has interest.

Trying to decide which it is can drive you crazy, but it really shouldn't, Champ. It should be pretty clear cut. Either the prospect originally gave you time or didn't. There's nothing concrete in sales, but experience has shown me engagement is directly correlated to the chance of close.

The amount of time you have to invest in that prospect should also be a factor. If pitching means flying across the country and days of travel, you should be spending lots of time checking with your prospect beforehand. If your meeting is across the street, maybe you don't have to worry quite so much. It all comes down to your judgment and that of your sales manager (if he is worth a damn).

Outright rejection is a gift. Say what?! How could rejection be a gift? Because it prevents you from wasting time on a bad prospect. Outright rejection actually helps your closing ratio, your grade, because you know to wait for a better pitch. Why swing at an outside pitch? Better to wait for one to come right down the middle.

Back to "Secondhand Lions." Finally the fourth salesman "Krafted" his pitch around the solution he invented. Yeah, I know it should be "Crafted" but then the acronym would have been S.I.C.C. not S.I.C.K. A little creative license never hurt anyone, Champ. Anyway, the salesman got away from his stupid script and crafted his plan just for that particular solution and the influencers he knew would weigh in on the deal.

It was kind of like Lincoln winning the Republican nomination by controlling the variables combined with second-graders singing in the pageant with no music. And if you have no idea what that means go back and read Chapters 2 and 5! The salesman controlled the variables of Huck, Garth and Walter, and created the pitch based around their needs instead of following a canned one. Imagine that, he got the sale. Cash money in hand and no gunshot wounds.

So the question is, why aren't you being S.I.C.K. each and every time you have a prospect? Let the self-fulfilling prophecies and excuses begin! "Well, I'm so busy making calls I don't have time to prepare like that!" "The prospect didn't tell me what they wanted!" "I didn't want them to cancel my meeting so I didn't check." "I'm afraid I will get it wrong." Blah, blah, blah, blah.

S.I.C.K. preparation is just like homework when you were in second grade. There were a million things that got in the way of getting it done, most of which you invented. Homework never went away though, and it had to be done in order to get a good grade. The same goes for S.I.C.K. preparation.

You have to do it after hours. You have to do it on your own time to truly excel with it. Yes, you have to work at your job when you aren't actually in the office. Some of you may think that is too much to ask, that the company isn't paying you for those hours. How penny-wise and pound-foolish can you be? Especially if you are a commissioned salesperson?

Aside from the silly "they aren't paying me for those hours" excuse, what else do you have to do? Watch some stupid show on TV? Would it be that hard to watch just a half-hour less every night? Or if you are really addicted, to do research during commercials? Seriously, have you ever counted how many commercials there are in a football game? You could paint the Sistine Chapel!

Do you have to take care of your kids? Well, there's no getting around that one! But how about 30 minutes after they go to bed or before they get up? If preparing so you can sell more and make more isn't taking care of your kids, what is?

Bottom line (and if I only had a dime for every time I've said this to a salesperson ...) is if you want it, you will find a way. Doing lots of S.I.C.K. homework won't be a chore. It will be a step toward laughing all the way to the bank.

And that's what Selling Like a Second-Grader is all about; refocusing so you can have all the things you want out of sales. So you can love your job and make more than ever. Study and practice the lessons and you will.

Final homework assignment:

Do S.I.C.K. preparation for your next 20 sales meetings. Compare the closing ratio to 20 where you prepared like S.H.I.T.

Acknowledgements

So many people helped me with this book – knowingly or not! First thanks goes to Bob Rose, my dad who sold oil like a champ to keep us fed, sheltered and flush in O.P. t-shirts. He taught me a ton about selling and service in the process. Next up is my late father-in-law, Russ Serzen, a great salesman in his own right. His "gonna happen" advice always stuck with me. So has his daughter Alison. She's far more than a wife. She is truly my partner who has always encouraged me to chase my dreams.

Professionally, my "extended family" at McMurry, Inc. has helped me grow beyond my expectations. I've learned from every one of the amazing people who work there, especially Chris and Preston McMurry who have been sage advisers. My boss Fred Petrovsky deserves the most credit for never firing me (even though it was warranted at least once) and being my "Zen" guru. Amy Shepard shows me the definition of dignity and tenacity every day. Thanks for encouraging me to, "do it" and write this book.

Many thanks also go to Christy Orders, who edited my first three chapters – an enormous task! Darlene Bush Tucker wore out several red pens editing the entire manuscript; twice no less. Her encouragement helped me realize my work just might be worth reading. Bob Wilcox was good enough to lay out the book perfectly in exchange for a case of Pabst and some mountain bike riding lessons. See you on Trail 100 some time.

1 Zlatan Krisan and Paul Windschitl, "The Influence of Outcome Desirability on Optimism," *Psychological Bulletin*, 2007, Vol. 133, No 1, 95-121

2 Goodwin, Doris Kearns. *Team of Rivals*, (Simon & Schuster, 2005), pp 55.

3 Abraham Lincoln Presidential Library and Museum, "Interactive Timeline", www.alplm.org/timeline/timeline.html (Accessed July 15, 2007).

4Goodwin, Doris Kearns. *Team of Rivals*. (Simon & Schuster, 2005), 186.

5 Ibid, pp 240-241

6 Ibid, pp 241

7 Ibid, pp 219

8 Ibid, pp 248-249

9 Ibid, pp 252-254

10 Langer, E. J. "The Illusion of Control." *Journal of Personality and Social Psychology* (32:2), 1975: 311-328.

11 Ibid.

12 Ibid.

13 Ibid.

14 Merton, Robert. "The Self-Fulfilling Prophecy." Antioch Review, 8:2 (1948: June): 194.

15 diStefano, Theodore F. "Bear Stearns: Are the Directors at Risk?" *E-Commerce Times*, www.ecommercetimes.com/story/ Bear-Stearns-Are-the-Directors-at-Risk-62963.html (accessed May 19, 2008).

16 Rosenblatt, Susannah and Rainey, James. "Katrina Rumors." *Los Angeles Times*, www.latimes.com/news/nationworld/nation/ la-na-rumors27sep27,0,5492806,full.story?coll=la-home-headlines (accessed August 15, 2007).

17 Arden, Patrick. "Hoarding Epidemic hits US, New York." *Metro New York*, http://ny.metro.us/metro/local/article/Hoarding_ epidemic_hits_US_New_York/12314.html (accessed May 20, 2008).

18 Ibid.

19 Bryson, George and O'Malley, Julia. "Rumors of Rice Shortage Spur Daily Rush at Anchorage Stores." *Anchorage Daily News*, www.adn.com/anchorage/story/394730.html (accessed May 20, 2008).

20 Merton, Robert. "The Self-Fulfilling Prophecy." *Antioch Review*, 8:2 (1948: June): 200

21 Ibid.

22 Sonnenmoser, Marion. "Upstaging Stage Fright." *Scientific American Mind*. February/March,2006, Volume 17, Number 1.

23 Guskin, Harold. *How to Stop Acting*. (Faber and Faber, Inc., 2003).

24 Vohs, Kathleen, Baumeister Roy, and Ciarocco, Natalie. "Self-Regulation and Self-Presentation: Regulatory Resource Depletion Impairs Impression Management and Effortful Self-Presentation Depletes Regulatory Resources." *Journal of Personality and Social Psychology*. (2005, Vol 88, No. 4): 633

25 Wilson, Edward O. *On Human Nature*. (Harvard University Press, 1978, 2004) 92-93.

26 Geller, Robert J., MD, Rubin, Leslie L, MD, Nodvin, Janice T., BA, Teague, Gerald W., MD, Frumkin, Howard, MD, DrH, "Safe and Healthy School Environments." *Pediatric Clinics of North America*. (2007, Vol 54): 351-373

27 Ibid.

28 Learning Connection, The Value of Improving Nutrition and Physical Activity in our Schools, Action for Healthy Kids www.actionforhealthykids.org/pdf/Learning%20Connection%20-%20Full%20Report%20011006.pdf (accessed January 13, 2009).

29 Ibid.

30 Measures and Models for Predicting Cognitive Fatigue, Ames NASA Research Center

31 www.city-data.com/city/Prineville-Oregon.html (Accessed April 1, 2009).

32 National Teacher of the Year Finalist, Michael Geisen www.ccsso.org/content/PDFs/2008ORNTOYFAPP.pdf (Accessed March 30, 2009).

33 Bynner, Wittner, The Way of Life, According to Laotzu. (Perigee Trade 1986):11-18.

34 What is Servant Leadership? www.greenleaf.org/whatissl/index.html (accessed April 1, 2009).

35 National Teacher of the Year Finalist, Michael Geisen http://www.ccsso.org/content/PDFs/2008ORNTOYFAPP.pdf (Accessed March 30, 2009): 8.

36 Conger, Cristen. Why was Alaskan Fishing Named the Most Dangerous Job in the World? http://adventure.howstuffworks.com/outdoor-activities/fishing/fish-conservation/responsible-fishing/alaska-fishing.htm (Accessed May 3, 2009).

37 National Compensation Survey: Occupational Wages in the United States, June 2006 http://www.bls.gov/ncs/ocs/sp/ncbl0910.pdf (Accessed, May 3, 2009)

What do you do with a BA in Creative Writing? Go into media of course! Chad Rose started his career in media as an unpaid intern at the Fox affiliate in Tampa, Florida. After stints as video tape editor and news producer, he gave into the inevitability of a sales career and cut his teeth in sales pedaling packaged health news stories to local news directors across the country. Gaining an MBA along the way, now Chad consults on content marketing strategies for Fortune 1000 companies and major health systems across the United States and Canada for McMurry, Inc.

Today you will find him researching psychology that applies to sales in his never ending quest to improve the performance of himself and his team. He also enjoys learning about history, especially the Civil War.

Chad is an Ironman triathlete, still rocks out as the lead singer of The Toads, has written two novels and of course this book. Other than that, he's a proud dad and sneaks skulls into his outfits whenever possible.

www.2ndgradeselling.com

Made in the USA
Charleston, SC
20 December 2012